"With *Extractivisms, Existences and Extinctions*, Markus Kröger has given us a searing critique of capitalist extractivism and its destruction of human and other webs of life. Arguing that we must embrace 'more than human' ways of seeing today's crisis, Kröger makes a signal contribution to ongoing struggles for planetary justice."

**Jason W. Moore**, *Binghamton University, USA, is the author of* Capitalism in the Web of Life

"In this carefully researched and passionately argued book, Markus Kröger connects diverging strands of scholarship to delineate the contours of an 'existential political economy'; a mode of analysis fit to capture extractivism's essence as a machine that redistributes existences in such a way that the only things left are commodities ... and extinctions. A must read!"

**Mario Blaser**, *Memorial University, Canada*

"Markus Kröger offers a daring and sensible work, marked by epistemic ruptures inspired by Latin American Political Ontology and extensive fieldwork that spans several years and many journeys to the Brazilian Amazon. Utilizing consistent data in tandem with novel theorizing, this book analyzes the plurality of extractivisms while unpacking Cartesian labels to unravel the variety of existences being destroyed in our time. His personal testimony is masterfully combined with interviewees' statements; together vividly voicing the ways in which existences are extinguished by different modes of extractivism."

**Andréa Zhouri**, *Federal University of Minas Gerais, Brazil*

"A beautifully-written examination of rare depth that offers insight into the many layers of life within what are typically labeled simply 'resources.' Markus Kröger forces readers to see how plantation-style extraction threatens the existence of subsistence, spirits, memories and a range of possible futures."

**Wendy Wolford**, *Vice Provost for International Affairs, and Robert A. and Ruth E. Polson Professor of Global Development at Cornell University, USA*

# Extractivisms, Existences, and Extinctions

This book explores the existential redistributions that extractivist frontiers create, going beyond existing studies by bringing into the English-language discussion much of the wisdom from Latin American rural and forest communities' understandings of extractivist phenomena, and the destruction and changes in lives and lived environments they create.

The author explores the many different types of extractivism, ranging from agro extractivist monocultures to mineral extraction, and analyzes the differences between them. The existential transformations of Brazil's Amazon and Cerrado regions, previously inhabited by Indigenous people but now being deforested by colonizers who expand soybean plantations, are analyzed in detail. The author also compares extractivisms with the local and broader existential changes through global production networks and their shifts, produced by monoculture plantation-based extractivist operations. Anchored in the author's own ethnographic data and comparison of lessons across multiple extractivist frontiers, the chapters integrate the many accounts of violence, and onto-epistemic and moral changes in extractivist enclaves, looking at these with the help of political ontology. The book offers details on how to characterize and compare different types and degrees of extractivisms and anti-extractivisms.

This transdisciplinary book provides new organizing concepts and theoretical frameworks for starting to analyze the unfolding natural resource politics of the post-coronavirus era, the advancing climate emergency, and the ever more chaotic multi-polar world. It will be of interest to students and scholars in the fields of international development, global value chains, political economy, Latin American Studies, political ecology, and international trade, as well as anyone engaged with the practical and political issues related to globalization.

**Markus Kröger** is Associate Professor of Global Development Studies and Academy of Finland Research Fellow in the Faculty of Social Sciences at the University of Helsinki, Finland. He is the author of *Contentious Agency and Natural Resource Politics* (2014), *Iron Will: Global Extractivism and Mining Resistance in Brazil and India* (2021), and *Studying Complex Interactions and Outcomes Through Qualitative Comparative Analysis: A Practical Guide to Comparative Case Studies and Ethnographic Data Analysis* (2021).

**Rethinking Globalizations**
Edited by **Barry K. Gills**, *University of Helsinki, Finland* and **Kevin Gray**, *University of Sussex, UK.*

This series is designed to break new ground in the literature on globalization and its academic and popular understanding. Rather than perpetuating or simply reacting to the economic understanding of globalization, this series seeks to capture the term and broaden its meaning to encompass a wide range of issues and disciplines and convey a sense of alternative possibilities for the future.

**Multiplicity**
A New Common Ground for International Relations?
*Edited by Justin Rosenberg and Milja Kurki*

**Global Justice and Resource Curse**
Combining Statism and Cosmopolitanism
*Frank Aragbonfoh Abumere*

**Extractivisms, Existences and Extinctions**
Monoculture Plantations and Amazon Deforestation
*Markus Kröger*

**Beyond the Global Land Grab**
New Directions for Research on Land Struggles and Global Agrarian Change
*Edited by Gustavo de L. T. Oliveira, Juan Liu and Ben M. McKay*

**Why Globalization Matters**
Engaging with Theory
*Edited by Barrie Axford*

For more information about this series, please visit: https://www.routledge.com/Rethinking-Globalizations/book-series/RG

# Extractivisms, Existences, and Extinctions

## Monoculture Plantations and Amazon Deforestation

**Markus Kröger**

Routledge
Taylor & Francis Group
LONDON AND NEW YORK

First published 2022
by Routledge
2 Park Square, Milton Park, Abingdon, Oxon OX14 4RN

and by Routledge
605 Third Avenue, New York, NY 10158

*Routledge is an imprint of the Taylor & Francis Group, an informa business*



*British Library Cataloguing-in-Publication Data*
A catalogue record for this book is available from the British Library

*Library of Congress Cataloging-in-Publication Data*
Names: Kröger, Markus, 1980– author.
Title: Extractivisms, existences and extinctions : monoculture plantations and Amazon deforestation / Markus Kröger. Description: Abingdon, Oxon ; New York, NY : Routledge, 2022. |
Series: Rethinking globalizations | Includes bibliographical references and index. Identifiers: LCCN 2021023625 (print) | LCCN 2021023626 (ebook) | ISBN 9780367610302 (hardback) | ISBN 9780367610333 (paperback) | ISBN 9781003102977 (ebook) Subjects:
LCSH: Natural resources—Social aspects—Brazil. | Agricultural industries—Social aspects—Brazil. | Mineral industries—Social aspects—Brazil. | Indigenous peoples—Brazil—Social conditions. | Environmental protection—Brazil—Citizen participation. | Political ecology—Brazil. | Economic development—Environmental aspects—Brazil. | Brazil—Environmental conditions—21st century. | Brazil—Economic conditions—1985– Classification:
LCC HC187.5 .K75 2022 (print) | LCC HC187.5 (ebook) |
DDC 333.70981—dc23 LC record available at https://lccn.loc.gov/2021023625LC ebook record available at https://lccn.loc.gov/2021023626

ISBN: 978-0-367-61030-2 (hbk)
ISBN: 978-0-367-61033-3 (pbk)
ISBN: 978-1-003-10297-7 (ebk)

DOI: 10.4324/9781003102977

Typeset in Times
by KnowledgeWorks Global Ltd.

# Contents

# Figures and Tables

## Figures



## Table

# Acknowledgments

This book is based on many encounters and experiences, discussions, and walks I have had with numerous people in different parts of the world. I am deeply grateful for the opportunities to exchange ideas with all of you. It would be impossible to mention in this short section all the people who have helped in different forms in the process behind this book.

First, I would like to thank the inhabitants of the Amazon in Brazil and Peru, whose insights and lived experiences were essential for starting to think through existences in the way proposed in this book. I am especially grateful to Claudio Ferreira for his friendship, and sharing his lived worlds with me. I would also like to thank the several Indigenous and other traditional forest-dwelling people and populations in the Amazon, who welcomed me and shared their concerns and worldviews with me, offering answers to many questions and changing the way existences should be understood. I would like to thank all those who gave their time for interviews and showing me around.

The ideas herein benefited from commentaries by participants in several seminars and conferences to presentations. I would like to thank Eduardo Gudynas, Mario Blaser, and Marisol de la Cadena for commentaries and discussions in several events in Peru and Finland on Political Ontology and extractivisms. I am also grateful to the reviewers of the book proposal, and the several in-depth discussions around this book idea with Barry Gills. The World-Ecology conferences and comments by Jason W. Moore were also essential, thank you for your time. In Finland, I benefited from critical discussions with Teivo Teivainen about metapolitics and agency, and Anja Nygren about Latin American political ecology and ontology. Likewise, I would like to thank several of my other colleagues at University of Helsinki in Global Development Studies, including especially Ossi Ollinaho, as well as Nidia González, Eija Ranta, Maija Lassila, and

Aili Pyhälä. Reflections while discussing with Maria Ehrnström-Fuentes, Inkeri Aula, Tero Toivanen, Mikko Pyhälä, Ilari Sääksjärvi, and Pirjo Virtanen were also important in expanding the understanding of the diversity of life at stake in different forests of the world. I am also thankful to Julia Dahlberg for the discussion around existences while collecting cloudberries and walking in Finnish swamps and forests.

In Brazil, I am grateful to Adriana Margutti, Biancca Scarpeline de Castro, Cristina Silva, Tião de Moises, Pablo Carrasco, Livaldo Sarmento, and Mika Rönkkö for the exchange of ideas and logistical help. I am also grateful to Mika Mäkeläinen, Caio Vilela, and Joceli for sharing a trip across the Amazon with me in 2019, during which some of the material for this book was collected in Mato Grosso. In Peru, I would like to thank Luciano Ávila for logistical help, and Matti Salo for both contacts and sharing ideas. Sanna Komi helped in the transcription of some of the Spanish language interviews I conducted and offered valuable comments.

Lastly, I would like to thank Saana Hokkanen for excellent research assistance, reading through, and reviewing a vast array of literature and offering insightful comments on the chapter drafts. These comments and discussions have been essential for building this book. I am also extremely grateful to Sophia Hagolani-Albov, who helped by giving comments to the book chapters, editing them in detail, and in countless other issues. My partner Jenni Munne supported me throughout the intense writing process in countless ways, and this book would not be possible without her support, commentaries, and help.

# Prologue

I first arrived in 2005 to the city of Belém at the estuary of the great Amazon rivers. I was to spend the next several months helping the Brazilian rubber tappers and other traditional forest-dwelling populations through development cooperation projects, which sought to preserve and improve the quality of life in the forests they inhabited. A large development cooperation project funded by Finland was ending. This project had promoted the creation and improvement of multiple-use conservation areas in the Amazon. My task was to help look for and develop projects so similar work could continue.

During my first night in the Amazon, I had a profound experience. I woke with a start in the middle of the night, horrified. I had a vivid dream that I was in a boat traveling upriver. We went deeper and deeper looking for the heart of the Amazon, propelled forward as if called by someone in the rainforest. When we finally arrived at the headwaters of the river, to my deep horror, I saw that all the huge, ancient trees had been recently cut, and all that remained were the stumps. These majestic trees had been killed; they were no more. The grief was deep and heart-felt. When I woke up in the middle of that moist night in Belém, I wondered if the forest, the ancient trees, had been communicating with me. Was there someone trying to call for help, asking me to arrive as soon as possible to some place that had to be found?

In the coming days, I visited the verdant Rodrigues Alves botanical garden in the middle of the buzz of the Belém metropolis area, where the offices of forest-dwellers' organizations were located. The air in the garden, which resembled an Amazonian forest, was cool and refreshing to breathe. There, I was briefed about my impending journey upriver to the Santarém region at the confluence of the Tapajós and Arapiuns rivers. The boat ride takes about three days, but this first time I took a plane. Meandering rivers and green forests spread all around during the journey west from Belém, showcasing from the air the beauty of this magnificent forest.

Upon arriving to Santarém's Alter do Chão, the picturesque, unique riverside village, and lake beach paradise, I started to look for a place to stay. First, I was offered a temporary lodging in a large house with tall walls, and a big German shepherd, who hunted and ate lizards, and guarded the house. After a couple of weeks, a man selling his artisanal works at the village center square approached me while I was passing and said to me in Portuguese, "The entity inside of me has been communicating with the entity inside of you already for a long while. I know that you are looking for a place to stay, and I know of a house for us to rent together." Although I was surprised by this frank approach and out-of-the-blue encounter, it felt completely natural, and we went to look at this house and we rented it. The man I moved into the house with was called Leopardo; he goes by many names, but I will use this, the first nickname he had when I met him in 2005. While living with him, I learned that he was a unique kind of person, as he mixed being an Indigenous "shaman," an afro-spiritual Umbanda "bishop," and a capoeira teacher. He was very stable and peaceful, and always walked with good posture and confidence, with power. The next months were an immersion into another kind of world, or more accurately a multitude of different parallel existences, a world of worlds. For me, this time brought a personal understanding and up-close experience of how there can be multiple, overlapping existences and worlds within the same apparent space, all with their own logics and energies of operation, of which one knows very little of without personally feeling them through the experience of living through them and being immersed in them.

On one night, while spending time in the village central square, I said to my friend Leopardo that it would be fantastic to re-live how the Indigenous people had lived in that same spot, hundreds of years ago, before the arrival of Europeans. He asked me to step closer to the riverside bank, which overlooked an island of white sand and forests, with a holy hill behind. He then asked me to close my eyes, take off my shoes, step onto the sand, and then open my eyes and look across to the island. I saw the thatched roofs of the buildings on top of the sand, and looked at the slowly flowing shallow river that softly bent where we stood. If one could suspend their disbelief by ignoring the two streetlights in view, they could be transported to a different time. This was the same view as had been there for a long time. It was a vision of peace and tranquility that went beyond time. It was suddenly easy to imagine how life had been in that spot before our time.

*Figure P.1* The view across the river to the peninsula Ilha do Amor (Island of Love), in Alter do Chão.
Source: Photo taken by the author.

Little by little I became immersed in a new way of sensing things in this wonderful place, observing events and feelings that were novel to me. I came to understand how little I had known or understood before about the world. I was 25 years old, and had passed a couple of years studying and traveling around South America and Asia, and had lived through quite a bit, but this experience was something quite different, and was felt on a deeper level. At times there were very pressing sensations, which vanished when we had figured out what the exact reason was for the imbalance, and we were able to do something about it. For example, once we both experienced a pressing, negative feeling for several days and we could not pinpoint where or why it had come. We started to discuss what might be behind these feelings, and decided we need to go out to explore the town to see what was happening. While we walked around the town, we learned that a young boy, who had become homeless, was being kicked at the beach as he had possibly tried to take something from a restaurant to sustain himself. Leopardo knew him. In this town, there were not street kids, but rather beach kids, living on the sandy stretches and sleeping in hammocks. We took the boy to the house we were renting, and allowed him to stay there until his issues got sorted out. This immediately eased the feelings, and made the pressure vanish. Leopardo explained that the negative energies sent by that boy were very strong, and made the emotions change in the village. Whatever the reason for the change in sensations, be it that or the fact that we had simply directed our attention toward trying to help someone, I do not know, but we were relieved by the change, feeling again at ease. The next time I saw the boy on a visit 14 years later, by then he had his own family and a boat, and gave me and Leopardo a ride on the river.

Leopardo passed many lessons to me that stemmed from his Afro-Brazilian and Amazonian Indigenous roots, by living through similar strong experiences where one immerses into omnipresent and pressing emotions. I observed things that some could call mystical, but whose presence anyone who has stayed longer in the Amazon forests might know, feel, or at least have heard of. There was something curious to Leopardo and the world we were inhabiting. At night, he lit candles in the house garden while talking to spirits and ancestors. Dogs barked ten meters behind him seemingly at someone, as if someone would be walking there, although I could not see anyone. He said that an entity followed him around, and the dogs barked at that entity, but he did not mind.

There is so much to this world that people who have lived mostly within the modern, virtual, and imagined spaces of Western societies know little about. It is at the frontiers, like in Alter do Chão, or more precisely, when living with others who are in distinct yet simultaneously present realities and worlds, where one can get a glimpse into a receding, but still present multitude of worlds. During this time, I was made clearly aware that multiple and often contradictory worlds can and do co-exist. This was not simply an intellectual understanding, but a personal experience.

I returned to the region and the same town many times after 2005, and each time the town was more modernized and further developed for tourists. I was sad to see that the riverbanks were fortified with concrete, and several of the huge, ancient mango trees that had given us fruit, were cut down to make space for a concrete pavilion. There was a shift from the older world, which before could still be envisioned by merely overlooking a streetlamp. The new scenery made it increasingly hard, if not impossible to make the same wholesale journey back to a different time of being. The space, which once had such potential for this overlapping of times, was being transformed. Interestingly enough, in addition to the change in the look of the place, there was also a marked change in the time. By this I mean the time, which ran before without notice or worry, was no longer. Time itself had shifted toward a faster-paced, more linear rhythm, organized by the growing number of restaurants, hotels, tours, and other commercial endeavors that catered to the increasing number of tourists. In the intervening years the town had been named as the number one beach destination in Brazil by the *Guardian*, so it was no wonder that it was attracting a new kind of global and national attention (McOwan 2009).

Not only was the town changing, but, perhaps even more importantly, the forests that surround the Santarém region were also changing. In 2005, my friend said he saw Blairo Maggi, the soy emperor of Brazil, stepping out of a riverside restaurant in Santarém. He swept the air with his hands, and said to the gathered crowd of local decision makers that soon this whole region will be covered with soybeans. And so, it was …

In subsequent years, enormous swaths of rainforests were deforested, huge trees were razed to the ground, and replaced by soybean plantations, promulgated by the newly built Cargill port in the city by the Amazon river. Local activists and environmental organizations denounced the port construction as illegal, as the port was built on top of an ancient Indigenous cemetery—in a parallel to earlier times when the Christian central square of Alter do Chão had been built on top of the existing Indigenous village center. Those trying to denounce the illegalities of the soybean craze, the violence, and rural exodus, were either threatened by the *pistoleiros*, who were the hired guns of the large land grabbers, murdered, or placed under police protection. Some were mugged and threatened, and had to move away for their safety. Some were even driven out of the town at gunpoint. Friends of mine were caught up in the fray. The soy barons erected mansions with tall stone walls at all the best spots along the riverside in the growing town. No longer a fishing village of a few thousand people, the area had grown rapidly into a conglomeration ten times larger, complete with shantytowns, and all the rising problems typical to urban destitution in Brazil.

Returning to the village in 2007, 2011, 2018, and 2019, I never again had the same kinds of experiences as in 2005. The magical, other-worldly sensations and experiences were just not there anymore with the same intensity or force. It felt as if the spirits, energies, entities, or whatever one would like to call such forces, had moved along, looking for more peaceful, less disturbed areas. There is so much to this world, and its laws and existences, that we know very little of, and in many cases, we are not even aware of how little we know. This ignorance or lack of recognition of what we do not know leads to the loss of countless lives, webs, and spectrums of life. Even the existences that are not visibly obliterated can be lost as the places they are tied to are transformed into something else. Places are burned down, cut, built over, and changed so drastically that it is difficult to even see the place as it was before, even when observing an area of hundreds of square kilometers from an airplane, or for days on end from a bus window. This is a profound loss, and yet, the pace of destruction continues to accelerate around the world. Even the Amazon is not immune from being destroyed, with its rich and wide spectrum of trillions of lives.

I try to make sense of these changes, based primarily on my personal experiences of living, traveling, doing research, and feeling in different parts of South America, Finland, and India, but especially in the Amazon. This book is based on these personal experiences and understandings, not simply on more typical participant observation and field research.

Since 2005, as I traveled by road across the Amazon, I saw how areas that had been covered by thick forests were transformed in just a matter of years to endless horizons of soybeans, other plantations, and pastures. What are the vocabularies by which these events could and should be described? How can one adequately tell of the magnitude of losses—real, tangible losses of uncountable lives of the myriad life forms that lived in those forests? Many of us have borne witness to this destruction, but from afar, for example, through the news. This distance coupled with an inadequate vocabulary sterilizes these events. Is this destruction better understood as the losses of beings—sentient beings—or of energies and forces? Or should these losses be described and captured by something altogether different? Whatever the answer to this question may be, it is less important than being able to see and understand that these are events that have led to drastic changes in what exists, and what can exist, in different spaces and places. These transformations take place at many levels, including the social and symbolic level. They are also taking place in physical, tangible, and territorial spaces, which are interlinked with the social and symbolic levels. Places are transformed that are homes with their own worlds, which cannot be compensated as they are unique places with their own specific histories and presences. In this book, I explore how these changes are linked to expanding extractivisms, that is, how extractivisms extinguish and redistribute existences. Extractivism has been defined as "a particular way of thinking and the properties and practices organized towards the goal of maximizing benefit through extraction, which brings in its wake violence and destruction" (Durante, Kröger, and LaFleur 2021). I will start this book from this premise. In Chapter 2, there will be a further characterization of the different types of extractivisms and their degrees, and also examples of what kind of activities should not be called extractivist. This book explores what impacts and dynamics extractivisms have with existences.

There are changes, where not only a life is lost, but where the possibilities are lost for entire species, populations, entities, webs, and spectrums of life. These losses ravage particular places and territories. These changes affect the whole world because when particular places are lost, or radically altered by extractivist damages, even when they are on the other side of the globe, the outcomes affect everyone via global climate and ecological crises. These global level changes even affect those making the decisions and pushing extractivisms.

One may see that this is a change promulgated by shifts in forces. A shift in the mental, vocal, and physical actions of people, especially of certain, powerful people, located at key junctures in modern webs of value-creation, markets, and politics. During my field research trips since 2005, traveling across the region called MATOPIBA (referring to the first two letters of the states of Maranhão, Tocantins, Piauí, and Bahia), and the Cerrado-Amazon arc of deforestation running from Acre to Belém, I met people whose job it was to arrive first to a region slated to be colonized by the soybean, and their Southern Brazilian patrons. These people worked to organize the region through the land markets, by parceling the forest lands, creating the legal documents, arranging the sale of slots, and contacting would-be buyers. At the same time, they organized the production, logistics, and trade. They saw themselves as developers, and do-gooders, heralds of modernity and prosperity. While the Indigenous people were portrayed as ill-doers and obstructive as they sometimes blocked the "developers" access to forests. I met soybean farmers, who saw themselves as "producers," as benefactors to a world in need of food and feed. From a critical analytical perspective (Dowbor 2019), they could also be called "unproducers," as their extraction destroyed soils, by just extracting the nutrients, and leaving behind toxic dirt—the so-called production was just a short-lived mirage. Real production being work that results in improvements to the places, guided by agroecological and other soil enriching practices—giving back to land, while producing, and not simply extracting in a destructive manner. There is much to be unpacked about the labels that people take on and give to themselves. These labels need to be dismantled and transformed when building the post-extractivist world. Even if these agrarian extractivists recognized that they had themselves razed down thousands of hectares of forests to make space for plantations, this was characterized as unfortunate but necessary. They made the excuse that there was still a lot of forest left untouched by their activities. I visited the fields with these soy and corn extractors, and I noticed that even in their own field, they were constantly looking at their mobile phones—observing the price of soybean, and other market news. Their lived worlds were not the same, even though they were at the same physical spots where just a few years or decades ago Indigenous people and forest animals roamed. They were not living or experiencing the same world as had been there before, there had been a fundamental shift in the use and intention of the territory. Their world was more abstract, virtual, not-there, not in the present—unless it was directly related to how well their crops were growing, for example, checking to see if there was need for fertilizer, a new kind of pesticide, or looking at the upcoming rains. There was a lot of time and attention given to planning for future expansions, and observing the land markets further away at the frontier, where good deals could still sometimes be found. These agrarian extractivists were focused on building larger silos to store the feed, while waiting for the best prices to sell the grains, and installing new corn ethanol facilities to make more use of and profits from the corn cover crop. They lived in the markets, whereas the Indigenous people lived in and with the forests—this description itself is a modern conceptualization of separating humans and nature, which Amazon Indigenous people do not even have.

In the northern parts of Mato Grosso state in Brazil, south of the Santarém region, there had been mostly nomadic gatherers, hunters, and fishers present until the 1970s. I spoke to the remnants of the Panará and other Indigenous peoples in an attempt to try and make sense of the genocidal policies that made the Panará almost extinct. I attempt to document what I heard from people living in the place. I spent several years in total in South America, meeting with forest and rural communities sometimes briefly and sometimes for more prolonged interactions. I will try to connect my experiences with the experiences and insights of others, especially in South America, regarding different types of highly destructive "natural resource" extractions and extractivisms. I will explore the existential transformations, redistributions, annihilations, and changes to existences that are created by different extractivisms, for example, the redistributions that the agro-extractivist soybean plantations create in the Amazon and Cerrado forests. How should these transformations be understood and conceptualized? What concepts can be used, in parallel with political economic analyses of power relations in agrarian markets, to do justice to the full sphere of existences and lives at stake and being lost in these processes? This book is an exploratory journey into these questions, offering an existential take on political economies.

# Introduction

## Introducing existences, extractivisms, and extinctions

The title concepts of this book refer to existences, extractivisms, and extinctions, but what do they mean and how are they related? Mostly extractivisms signify expanding annihilations and even extinctions. They are the capture of "resources" and the lives that compose or depend on these, or are destroyed or displaced as collateral damage of the extraction. Besides this, extractivisms also expand a radically less varied selection of life forms, which are expanded on top of the destroyed places, and replicated, cloned, and copied by the millions. These millions include particular crop varieties, animals (also some humans), as well as some unwanted species that come along, such as pests. These redistributions of existences cascade globally in the processing chains of extracted commodities, causing similar redistributions of existences across the chain, continuing even after the commodity is consumed, in continued disruptions that arise when dealing with the waste products. An example is the soybean-broiler-slaughterhouse-fast food-waste chain, which is just one of many destructive chains a commodity like soybeans could follow. Yet, these political economic dynamics at the local and global scales are not the whole story. There is much more that is transformed. This becomes clear when proper attention is given to Indigenous understandings of reality. One should not fall into the trap of making an account of existences only through modern Western lenses, looking at "ecosystems" or "biodiversity," but in fact, one should challenge these concepts, giving more space for Amazonian Indigenous and other non-or transmodernist understandings of what happens.

I will begin to answer the above question in its broader, political ontological understanding from a territorial viewpoint, based on my own experiences growing up and living in Finland. I come from a

DOI: 10.4324/9781003102977-1

country of forests, or at least a country where the tree cover is still very extensive. In the last few centuries, the forest has occupied the central role in Finnish commerce and society. In fact, I have found many similarities between the Amazon and Finland. There is something in forested landscapes that seems to create similar kinds of webs of existences and understandings. In Finland, I had heard tales and stories of forest spirits and communication with forests, which were not only from a long forgotten or discarded past, but that have persisted into fairly recent times. What I heard from Finland was similar to the kind of non-modernist forest understandings that I encountered in Brazil. In this book, I am particularly interested in the worlds within forests, and what happens to these worlds when forests are lost, removed, fragmented, degraded, deforested, and are transformed into pastures, farmlands, mines, roads, railroads, dams, reservoirs, and different kinds of logging or forestry areas.

The ways people interact with other living beings and their surroundings change over time and according to the circumstances of those times. Until the 1920s, according to the records of the Finnish National Archives, the ability to communicate with forest spirits or elves was the most important skill a person could have when going to the forest in many parts of Finland, especially, in the East (Letonsaari 2009). Folkloric researchers have documented and even drawn maps of where different kinds of spirits or elves (in Finnish *haltia*) lived, and their characteristics, based on the locals' accounts of the forest. As mentioned, until the 1920s, these accounts were full of speech about spirits and non-modernist forest entities or forces and dynamics. Not coincidentally, in my view, the 1920s and 1930s marked a period with an unforeseen rise of industrial forestry in Finland, when new factories were erected to make Finland a core part of the growing international forestry capitalism. Finland provided wood, especially, for the burgeoning German imperialist needs, within the pre-World War II struggle between Germany and the United States for world hegemony (see Koponen and Saaritsa 2019; Kuisma 2006; Toivanen 2018).

A growing number of forests were cut down and, more importantly, peoples' mentalities started to shift about the way they needed to interact with the forest. Previously, it was quite common to ask for a permission when entering the woods (a feature I found to still exist among several of the residents of the Amazon). Territorial shifts in landscapes seem to be linked with changes in what is seen as existing, a transformation that seems to go both ways. A marked sign of this is when key vocabularies and words change in a way that gives words new meanings, which befits and justifies a new system of forest use. These shifts can serve to make the potential violences of the shift less obvious or even hide them, which makes it harder or even impossible to fathom, represent, or recognize the possible non-modernist webs of lives and forces. These non-, other-than, more-than, or trans-modernist ways of talking about existences, or being (with) and communicating (with), or relating to forces, also represents something broader.[1] They are connected to different ways of being in the web of life, they are different cosmologies, which are rooted in distinct territorial practices. These forces or spirits are not separate from so-called material being. This becomes visible, when seeing how the expulsion of Indigenous peoples from their "lived environments" (see Taylor 2015), are causally linked with genocides, ethnocides, and ecocides (see Dunlap 2020), where the loss of non-modernist forces and spirits relates to the vanishing or radical redistribution and rearrangement of whole webs of existences, practices, species, cultures, livelihoods, sustenance possibilities, and so forth.

Existences, in their fullest understanding, are intimately linked with destructions caused by extractivisms, such as deforestations. For example, after an area has been deforested the forest spirits might not even be in the area anymore. By this I mean, if the being of these spirits is tied to the existence of old-growth forests, but then the trees are cut down the spirit might be gone along with the trees. The kind of changes in vocabularies can also be a sign of changed homologies between symbolic and physical spaces. When forest spirits are not mentioned anymore, or respected, this might mean that the forests, and their spirits, no longer exist in the same manner, as there is no longer a spatial homology, but instead a rupture caused by death in one or both spaces. Forces and spirits that once were embedded in their territories, which are no longer due to deforestation, often become forgotten in the language. Noting such discursive transformations can be important to try to detect the oncoming, potentially irreversible, and destructive redistributions of existences. Besides understanding the exact causal patterns, it is also essential to understand and note the overall changes. By this I mean the great transformation from one kind of lived world and environment to a more extractivist mindset and practice in relation to a given forest area.

The Political Ontological discussion in the Andes has noted how the current technologies and pace of extraction are more destructive for existences than prior extractions. De la Cadena (2015, 273) describes how "prospecting for Andean gold in the current millennium is different, for new mining technology demands the destruction of the mountain from which minerals are being extracted," which is "extremely polluting environmentally and represents the ultimate threat to earth-beings: the mountains that they also are and exceed faces nothing less than their destruction." This could also be interpreted to mean the destruction of this particular Andean relation, which I see as one example of an inherently anti-extractivist relational world. In similar relational worlds around the planet, a tree, bear, lichen, or mountain—not all, but some of them—can also be seen as being the force themselves, that is the spirit or actor that exists in these entities. These understandings are a challenge for the extractivist understandings. This can be illustrated with the example of a tree, which in a non-reciprocal, flattening, and extractive understanding would simply be seen as a source of wood. An essential aspect in transforming animist ways of relating in the web of life involves changing the existing relational worlds and communities between humans and other-than-human actors. In extractivist pushes, as well as in expanding modern religions, there is a tendency to try to transform, for example, what de la Cadena calls earth-beings into objects of human subjects. As a counter or an opposite to this, de la Cadena (2015, 207) describes a situation where "they are together and as such are place." I see the kind of relations that avoid the human subject or nature object dichotomy and appreciate being closely attuned to particular places and territories, as an antidote to extractivist properties, practices, and ways of thinking.

In this book, I will expand and try to unite the current ways of knowing about and discussing the losses in the spectrum of life, by linking most recent data on the worsening "biodiversity and ecosystem" situation to Indigenous and other, non-modern ways of knowing and being. Uniting these ways of knowing has been demanded across many disciplines and areas, e.g., in forest sciences (González and Kröger 2020), as well as in broad, overall evaluations of the current state of the planet by international organizations that are making an effort to draw also on Indigenous knowledge in addition to the standard Western scientific knowledge (see, e.g., IPBES 2019a).

Deforestation and turning forests into wood-sources for industrial forestry has occurred in pace with rapidly declining numbers of different species, both in terms of the losses in biodiversity and in the raw numbers of animals (IPBES 2019a; Kröger 2014; Marchak 1995). The landmark IPBES *Global Assessment Report on Biodiversity and Ecosystem Services* from 2019 extensively details the accelerating changes in what I call here existences. In addition, the report's draft chapters, e.g., Chapter 2.2. (IPBES 2019b, 5) also identify what has been created in these processes of redistribution:

> Indicators of the extent and structural condition of ecosystems, of the composition of ecological communities, and of species populations overwhelmingly show net declines over recent decades; most of the exceptions are themselves symptoms of damage (e.g., the biomass of prey fish has increased, but this is because humanity has harvested most of the bigger fish that prey on them…)

The situation has grown considerably worse in the past decades. New academic fields, such as extinction studies, environmental humanities and multispecies studies, have highlighted the massive and unparalleled scale of death today (Rose et al. 2017). Rose (2011) argues also that the quality of death-life cycle has changed, as the poisoning of animals, e.g., transforms the natural cycle where death feeds future life, as poisons accumulate in the food chains of beings (Rose 2011). Destructive processes, like those described in this book, transform landscapes and existences at a grand scale, and as a result of destructive process our imaginary of certain concepts like wilderness does not always match the reality of what still exists. While wilderness might often be thought of as something that is vast and still exists somewhere, tropical forest loss rates have actually tripled during the 2010s "due to industrial logging, agricultural expansion, fire and mining" (IPBES 2019b, 6). These large-scale destructions of lived environments, including the rapid increase in extinctions, are being termed an "ecocide" by some scholars and global environmental activists (Stop Ecocide n.d.). There is a concerted push to make ecocide a punishable crime. This would mean that heads of states, corporate directors, and other actors caught engaging in activities that cause this large-scale destruction could be prosecuted under the jurisdiction of the International Criminal Court (ICC) (Higgins et al. 2013; Lindgren 2018). Brazil's Jair Bolsonaro has become perhaps the best-known example and target in the rising demands for making powerholders responsible for their acts against the environment. Raftopoulos and Morley (2020, 1632–1633) argue that "Bolsonaro's policy, supported by Brazilian business sectors, to open up the region at any cost, is in line with the criteria set out in the preamble of the Ecocide Act with regard to the aiding, abetting, counseling, and procuring of the systematic ecocide of the Amazon."

Raftopoulos and Morley (2020) use the term extractivist imperialism to describe the so-called developmental actions of the Bolsonaro regime. These processes are the key drivers of the rising global extinctions, as noted by IPBES (2019b, 6), "the rate of species extinction is already at least tens to hundreds of times higher than it has averaged over the past 10 million years, and it is set to rise sharply still further unless drivers are reduced." Yet, little is done to avert this crisis, as regimes like Bolsonaro's are left unchecked by the international community.

The reason for these advancing crises lies in the structures, ontologies, and practices of the current modern, capitalist world-system (Dunlap and Jakobsen 2020), where for example forests are not valued, and deforestation is not checked. On the contrary, in this system commodity flows are prioritized, and enterprises are given a free hand to expand. Moreover, the existing legal frameworks support and largely protect the supreme and sacred value of the free flow of raw materials. I see that changing this trajectory should start from rethinking and revaluing lives, beginning with the ontological base of what is at stake here,. In this vein, legal scholars have criticized "the failure to establish an international crime against ecocide and its genocidal effects is a deeply rooted and unacceptable legal-epistemological disregard of alternative life-systems' intrinsic right to existence by international law" (Lindgren 2018, 525). It is at this conjuncture where the budding understanding of modernity's problems, and the concepts of extractivism and existences are essential for better understanding what is at stake, what is happening, and how to come out of these destructive processes. Non-modernist understandings and cosmologies are gaining more visibility, and campaigns around them are gaining traction, as the modern project is seen by many as having led, in spite of its many victories, to a planetary catastrophe (Blaser 2013), as evidenced by the climate emergency and overall environmental crises (Gills and Morgan 2020).

This is not just a continuation of millennia of so-called civilizations destroying forests and other natural habitats, but a markedly different process, with a particular history, and particular actors who are responsible for the increasing ecocides and redistributions of existences. There is now a considerable focus on the role of the rapid rise in human populations as the key beings who are now transforming the planet's stable Holocene period into the chaotic Anthropocene. This scholarship and attention have been correct in pointing out the rapid shifts in the distribution of existences between humans and all others. However, the Anthropocene concept lacks the ability to emphasize that some human groups have had far more power and responsibility for getting the planet into this situation (Moore 2016). In fact, much more precise concepts have been recommended to overcome the problems of the Anthropocene, and especially its neo-Malthusian connotations (Haraway 2015). For example, Capitalocene emphasizes the key role of corporate directors and owners, such as oil company bosses, in causing the climate crisis. For example, it would not be right or just to put the Amazonian nomadic Indigenous people into the same flat line with these capitalist bosses, as part of a "humanity" causing the problems as an imagined "we," which is often used by Westerners.

The current pace of destruction is at a very different magnitude than previous destruction, it is beyond comparison. IPBES (2019b, 8) stresses that due to the rising extinctions "[the] biosphere's capacity to adapt to possibly abrupt environmental change" may have already been severely compromised. Considering the scale and pace of losses today, in comparison to the past, it makes little sense to talk about thousands of years of "human-caused" ecocides. In fact, many people, such as the Indigenous peoples of the Amazon whose voices are reproduced in the excerpts from my interviews cited in this book, are actively working against the destruction. A further problem with the Anthropocene discussion is its anthropocentrism, whereby the ontological possibilities of understanding the whole spectrum of what is at stake are not easily captured, or are actively forgotten and brushed aside. Even the use of some common concepts can hide the range of existences affected by the destruction. These include such concepts as "biodiversity," which by its very character masses together species/beings/life, or "ecosystem," which frames environment as serving humanity and even humanity as separate from the environment. When these concepts are used in lieu of broader concepts it makes it more difficult to consider lives and life through a broader and less Euro-centric lens.

Even seemingly neutral concepts such as "species," as understood and reified in the Linnean taxonomy, have been heavily criticized. Carl von Linné's taxonomical project has been criticized for being a part of the modernist and Western, positivist worldview. This critique can be extended to biology as a discipline, which, in the sphere of existential politics, promotes and spreads an ontology on "species" across the web of life. The taxonomization of beings, giving them Latin names, has also been seen as the ontological root to discriminatory processes, such as speciesism, which values some animals less than others, leading to some animals being considered suitable targets for mass production, while others are suitable to be pets (see Singer 1995). Furthermore, evolution, and human modifications, keep changing "species" all the time, and thus broader conceptualizations, such as the web of life, with many beings, may be more suitable to refer to these changes, than the language of "species" now emphasized in scientific conservation and biology. In addition, Indigenous viewpoints on what these beings are differ radically from the "species" understanding, yet are downplayed still as less valuable, when what exists is catalogued. For these and other reasons I use rather the more encompassing concept of existences than the modern concepts such as "species." I do however also note what science says about species losses, changes, and modifications in relation to the expansion of extractivisms. This is done in parallel with the focus on existences and beings, instead of a flattening naming of a being by its Latin taxonomic name. The taxonomizing project runs into serious problems when noting what exists beyond what modern scientists typically cannot observe, and would not suffice for a fuller analysis of existences.

This loss in the web and spectrum of life is related to the process of annihilations and redistributions in terms of spirits, non-modernist forces, and practices. These losses are present and felt in practice at least by the people who understand the world through these forces. This is the case with many Afro-Brazilian Quilombo-communities, who understand that some waterfalls are more-than-waterfall forces. These forces do not only inhabit the waterfalls, but they are (also) waterfalls; this is different from saying that the waterfall would be "sacred" or "divine" in a (merely) non-material or religious sense of these words (see de la Cadena (2015) for a long critique of these concepts in the Andean context).

For someone from the Quilombo-community, to resist extractivism is to defend their very way of life. They are defending not only a specific place to live, but also a particular relation to work and in essence life itself. There are many spaces within the Quilombo territory, where the natural features contain more-than-modern entities. This means features like waterfalls and tree trunks do not only exist as such, but also carry other layers of existence. When a Quilombo is defending their landscape against extractivism these more-than-modern entities are also considered and defended. All their territory with its existing relations is as important to defend as their own houses and gardens. It is important to note that the Quilombos and others who live in a similar life-world have a different relationship to Oxum than the way in which modernity views religious beliefs. They know that Oxum exists, it is not simply "believing in" something as it would be interpreted through modernity's lens.[2] As de la Cadena (2015) opens up, in reference to Andean ways of understanding the community (*ayllu*) and existences, it is important to overcome such modern concepts as "spirit," belief, or god, as separate from the environment, and instead focus on conceptualizations that see these as the same and as overlapping (or non-dual). As de la Cadena (2015, 206) explains:

> Thus what in the world of travelers, anthropologists, politicians, and priests may be‘ “religion” is also *not* religion, but interactions with other-than-human entities that are neither natural nor supernatural, but beings that are *with* runakuna in socio-natural collectives that do not abide by the divisions between God, nature, and humanity.

The ontological specificities of the traditional population’s practices are understood by outsiders through a transmodern translation process and end up falling into the general category of locals defending of their existing territory. Yet, relegating this resistance to such a broad categorization hides important distinctions about the foundation on which the struggle is based (Kröger 2020a; 2021). This problem of translation is not unique in the Brazilian context and can be found in many outsider understandings of traditional populations and Indigenous resistance in many land conflicts in rural Latin America (and other places in the Global South).[3]

Thus, these extractivist conflicts are imbued with ontological conflicts. Extractivist actors and their logics are one way of being—that is there are particular sets of actors, who understand that some things exist according to a particular logic, while others are neglected in this logic. The encounter of these practices with other kinds of existences, and ways of ordering existences, is often rife with conflict and violence. One facet of the violence is what Viveiros de Castro (2004, 11) calls equivocation, which is, “a failure to understand that understandings are necessarily not the same, and that they are not related to imaginary ways of ‘seeing the world’ but to the real worlds that are being seen.”[4]

One of the biggest obstacles today for remodeling production patterns toward non-exploitative and non extractivist practices that would instead be based on reciprocity and care, is the non-recognition of existences. Animals in industrial meat factories are invisible. Forest loggers do not recognize and see all the animals who will lose their homes when the forest is cut. In fact, even scientists have become part of this in-built ignorance of modernity. Concepts, such as bioeconomy or biodiversity, flatten the existences into a mass, a volume, which does not emphasize, but hides the beings behind the terms that are considered to be more scientific by some.

In 2019, I gave a talk for primary school students in Finland about the Amazon. I asked what the Amazon is, and why should we care about it. The answers were surprising. The first and most common replies were, that the Amazon is the home of many different animals, who live there, and if it is destroyed, they will not have a home anymore. Climate, biodiversity, or other modern terms were missing from this healthy reminder of simply recognizing the lives at stake. Of course, this recognition might go well beyond the modern confines of sensing and understanding what exists. It is important to find vocabularies that are not inherently biased toward modernity's scales of valuation, but which open up and give space for the broad variety of what exists. One might see that there is a danger of straying into the grey zone of fake news, alternative facts, or post-truth politics by taking such a step. Thus, recognizing some key relational principles is even more important than arguing that this or that exists or does not exist. Thus, it is essential to look at processes that redistribute existences like extractivisms, and their antidotes.

Different kinds of practices and ways of acting are telling of broader patterns of being together with what exists. Asking a permission to enter to a particular place is a sign of reciprocity and care—of recognition and respect—the antidotes of the extractivist mindset. My friend Leopardo, who dedicates most of his time to what some would call spiritual practices and communicating with spirits in his Afro-Brazilian and Indigenous religions or cosmologies (if one wants to name them), advised me that it is always essential upon entering a place to first make a remark and recognize the spirits that could possibly live in the place. For example, going to whatever altar there is in a house, independent of the religion, and just being respectful and recognizing that there might be something one is not aware of here. Without taking sides or making a declaration of whether or not I think spirits, or other such entities exist, I want to observe what links these different traditions might have with forest cover, and the presence or absence of extractivist mindsets. I see this as an exercise of political analysis, a kind of political ontology, on what role different onto-epistemologies have in this world.

If the answer one gets to the question of whether one is welcomed to enter an area of the forest is negative, then one would be foolish to still enter there. To be clear, these answers are felt within a person, whether it be in their mind or their gut, rather than an overtly verbal answer. According to the old forest wisdoms and customs present in Finland as late as the early twentieth century, one should ask permission before setting up a camp to spend a night, and should not set up their tent or sleep on the forest paths. Before reading about these wisdoms, I had occasionally been afraid while sleeping alone in the woods, both in Finland and the Amazon. In the spirit of experimentation and without prejudice, I wanted to see if asking for a permission would make a difference to how I felt when I was out in the woods. So, the next time I set out to camp, I asked permission to enter the woods. When I heard a yes, I entered and began the task of selecting the site for my tent, always asking in my mind if this or that place would be ok. I received several noes, and my tent stayed in its bag. Finally, when I reached a certain place, I felt as though I received a yes rather than a no, and this is the place where I set up camp. After adopting this exercise, I have not had more troubled nights in the woods, but rather peaceful sleep. So, at least for me, there seemed to be wisdom in these practices of giving recognition and respect, and asking for permission.

Once after this, I went against a clear no that came when I questioned if I could set a camp on a beach of an island in the Baltic Sea. We had arrived late on a sailing boat; it was pitch dark and I was very tired and not up for looking for a place beyond the shore. I just wanted to pitch my tent on the beach and did not care that I got a no response deep down. However, I paid for my hubris and I woke up in the middle of the night covered in ants. I had pitched my tent on top of an ant nest, and they entered through a hole in my tent. I had to move the tent and did not rest as completely as I could have, had I initially listened to the answer. I do not know if these occurrences started to take place because I believed in them (I still do not feel like "believing" in them), or had come to know of such dynamics, or if they were there. Anyway, the answer to that question is not as important, as is the practical help I have gotten from drawing on the ancient wisdoms. I have only scant understanding of what is behind the reasons for these dynamics, but that is certainly borne of the limitations I have in understanding such things, and in using my person as a tool of investigation in the world. People who lived before the era of mass interruptions, of time sliced into a few seconds or minutes between checking emails from a smart phone, or reading social media incessantly, must have had a different kind of aptitude and inner silence to listen to and recognize these relations than people seeped in the processes of a modern information society. These notes above reflect my epistemological approaches to the subject of this book.

Etymologies of the key words to different cosmological orders, which are related to forests and what exists there, are revealing of those orders. For example, the word *väki* in Finnish currently refers to a group of human beings.[5] However, the etymology of this word refers to force, in a non-anthropocentric manner. Each nature element and force had its own *väki*. Different environments had different *väki*, which most commonly referred to a larger group of spirits or elves of different kinds, who were the guardian entities of particular environments, such as lakes, different places, or even elements. For example, fire and thunder had their *väki*, as did trees. Thus, if thunder struck a tree, then the wood of that tree had both the *väki* of thunder and of the tree. This wood carried this force when applied in different uses, and this force carried through the different iterations of the entity. For example, all the different *väki* could be incorporated by burning that piece of wood in a sauna, and then using that heated sauna for special purposes. This old meaning of force, whose character flows and fluctuates, and is not just coming from or referring to a group of humans, as in the current anthropocentric meaning, is still present in some sayings in Finnish. For example, in Finnish the word for violence is *väkivalta*, with *valta* meaning power. So, a use of power within the field of force, or in a forceful way, is violence. Use of power is something that goes against the natural order of force, *väki*, which refers to a natural and harmonious order of the world and environments, linked to the guardian spirits of particular, physical environments on which they depend.

Another interesting aspect of *väki*, as an example of a pre-modernist concept, is that the order present within *väki* was not dualist in the nature-society sense of Cartesian dualism. A fisher could ask for the force of waters to give force to them (in the form of a fish, which might not even be mentioned directly in the voiced request), as there was so much force or *väki* in water. Force flowed quite naturally, without any need of separating its parts, or it from humans.

Now imagine this order of different forces getting ruptured with the rise of capitalist and other extractivist mindsets, which either blind or ignorant to such old beliefs, clear-cut entire forests for logs, or to make tar, potash, or pulp, thus fundamentally changing the landscape (see Toivanen and Kröger 2019). It was believed that a frightened person was especially open to receiving *väki* of the different kinds of surrounding environments, which put the person and the community into an imbalance, which had to be restored by restoring the *väki* to their respective places in the cosmological balance. Seen from this perspective, the world of today is very much out of balance. For example, the force of fire, in the form of global heating, has become displaced and unbalanced. This is an explanation that emerged when I was in the Amazon, specifically that the forces of fire and ice were in global imbalance. I will talk more of these and other imbalances in the book. I was astonished to find very similar cosmologies in operation in the Amazon still to this day, as the way of understanding the world in pre-industrial forestry Finland.

The ontological and conceptual take away from this is that where there was force (*väki*), there were also possibly beings, entities, such as spirits, which might resemble humans, or they might be experienced as invisible or metaphorical energies, manifesting as volitions. They were guidelines on how to avoid negative developments and mental actions, such as being negative in a particular environment, from which forces could enter a human being and make that person sick. These kinds of animistic systems were common around the world. Their key difference is that they were not anthropocentric, but other existences could be seen to existing in their own right, outside of the service and convenience of humans. In the extractivist mindset, land and space are seen as non-valuable until they become part of human appropriation and use. The spaces where one speaks of forces and the web of life are antidotes to such spatial understandings. In these spaces, humans co-exist in interactions and conversations that exist on equal or shared terms with other-than-humans. These ways of being and the spaces which make them possible have become less common with the expansion of extractivist frontiers, which have destroyed environments, and alongside them, the symbolic systems and cosmologies linked to them. If these alternative cosmological orders with their notions of balance, care, and reciprocity (among others) carry some truth to them, just imagine the amount of sicknesses, body and mind in the forms of distress and unhappiness, that current extractivist practices entail for those who are destroying the environments (and, if existing, also and especially of the *väki* or spirit entities protecting and linked to them). The sickness and imbalances also extend to those witnessing the destruction.

As part of the *Rethinking Globalizations* book series, a key focus of this book is to contribute by linking the Latin American developments regarding extractivist expansions and their impacts on existences to their global impacts. I argue that what happens at the points of extraction, for example in the form of deforesting an area to be turned into a soybean monoculture plantation, not only directly affects the place-based existences in question, in all the above and other possible (and impossible) ways of imagining, but also produces a cascading global effect and thrust in terms of existential redistributions. The increased flow of cheap feed gives an impulse to develop and deploy similar, monocultural orderings around the world, for example of chicken and pig lives in animal farms. The feed is even specifically tailored to support this kind of re-ordering of livestock production. Thereafter, slaughterhouse workers' tasks are similarly monotonized and mechanized into routinized killing. The ordering of time and space takes place through the principle of serial killing, as fast and profitably as possibly, this logic placing aside all other, intervening, or non-needed existences.

Weis (2013) discusses the political economy of this agribusiness-monoculture complex, and its relations to the problems and peculiarities of global meat production. Weis (2013, 93), argues (as I also do even though I use partly different vocabularies) that we are currently living in a period where the scale and pace of destruction has reached new proportions, "[as] the incessant pressure to compete, grow, and accumulate under capitalism has pushed the expansion and simplification of farming landscapes to radical new extremes." Opening up how different forms of extractivisms are creating these new radical extremes, in terms of existences, can highlight the links of modernity and organized, systemic greed with destructions and reorganizations of whole webs and spectrums of lives and lived environments.

The bulk of this book will focus on making a contribution to the political economic literature, drawing on the above mentioned and other theoretical developments around political ontology and extractivism in Latin America, as well as my personal exposure(s). The violent destruction of existences is centrally linked to the expansion of a unitary logic of the capitalist (i.e., looking for profit and to profit as fast as possible, without caring about the costs) and a growth-centered feed-livestock complex. Existences are made similar and tied to each other when the system expands, which Weis (2013, 93) calls an "industrial grain-oilseed-livestock complex." Standardization and uniformity are imperatives for the "efficiency" and profitability of the extractivist feed-meat-complex. Weis (2013, 8) emphasizes "the loss of large volumes of usable nutrition," a point which Dowbor (2019) also makes in his book *The Age of Unproductive Capital* about the essence of agribusiness. Gudynas (2015) emphasizes that extractivism is an opposite to industry, or production of value in industrialization's connotation. In fact, extractivist expansions, such as agribusiness plantations, have much to do with causing massive losses, even in economic terms, or in terms like nutrition, which could be used not only by humans, but also by trees or plants, which cannot exist anymore in the same place in the same manner after the transition.

The territorial logic of extractivism is to radically transform the spaces it encounters. Under the extractivist logic, these spaces are considered as *terra nullius*, that is, they arc free to take and utilize in almost whatever way. This process was and still is the basis of white settler colonization of Indigenous worlds, as I will discuss, by citing the experiences of Indigenous people when meeting this violence. The logic itself is contrary to even starting to be able to think about interventions or changes based on first recognizing and building on what already exists in an area. As Weis (2013, 93) puts it, "rather than tailoring agricultural practices to bioregions, bioregions have to be transfigured to fit a set of practices and technologies." The prevalence of this agribusiness logic is a key explanation to understand why certain practices like agroecological agroforestry have not expanded over pastures, while destructive, short-term plantations are expanded (Ollinaho and Kröger 2021), or why Indigenous forest gardens are considered to be deforestation rather than forest enrichment by the Food and Agricultural Organization (FAO) (González and Kröger 2020). Moore (2015) argues that this logic has deep roots, being crystalized in the modern form around the long sixteenth century—that is, starting from the fifteenth century—and through the European colonial projects in the Atlantic and the Americas. The logic here is to make machines out of living beings, turning labor, including what Moore calls the unpaid labor of for example animals, into capital. In extractivist expansions, over 99 percent of the "stakeholders" are those who are not needed, who cannot be used in this process. In fact, where a monoculture plantation is established there is hardly anything, but the dirt left in the area, as the actions of establishing the plantation heavily impact the living biota of the existing soils. The species which are subject to monoculture expansion are brought from elsewhere, and what existed there before is just brushed aside, as the same space is needed for a new project. This space does not refer only to a landscape, but also includes the bodies of animals and humans.

Bodies that are targeted by an extractivist eye are also reshaped. The very quality and extension of life are reshaped, as bodies are turned into commodity vehicles in the cycle of capital that Marx (1976 [1867]) described, which is from money capital via commodity capital back to money capital. Importantly, redistributions of existences in these processes are not just about destruction of what is there during the process, but also about the production of new kinds of existences, for the benefit of ever-faster and more profitable capital accumulation. The example given by Weis (2013, 95–96) highlights this point well, "the increasing uniformity of animal bodies supports multiple objectives, abetting the standardization of animal enclosures, the speeding pace of slaughter lines, and the growing scale and consistency of meatpacking operations." Building on Weis (2013), to solve the myriad global problems, it would be essential to step away from the logic of standardizing and monotonizing production, species, and lived environments for the sake of capital accumulation. I will return back to these scalar, global dynamics of monoculture extractivisms later in this book. The key point here is that the objective and logic of especially agrarian, but also other forms of extractivism is uniformization, at a global scale. This logic is conflictive and contradictory with the respect and recognition for diversity in the spectrum of life. A key way to uncover this rupture is by trying to learn from people who exist at these points of encounter between these two logics.

## The methodological approach

The book presents and draws on direct quotes from my interviews with Amazon Indigenous and other populations. I will also offer space for other discourses, including from soybean farmers of European descent, to illustrate the different ontologies at work. These were not typical interviews, but based on participant observation in the field. These interviews were conducted when walking with the interviewees in areas targeted by or partially destroyed by different forms of extractivisms, and specifically asking them how they saw these changes. The discussions about non-modernist beings and worlds stems from these encounters, where people brought to my attention that modern terms do not convey their thoughts of what is at stake in the expansion of resource extraction, but that they understand it by other means, which need to be given much more attention. These ontological conflicts have been well theorized by South American Political Ontology (with capital letters, to separate this strand of political ontology from for example the Political Science tradition) (de la Cadena and Blaser 2018; Hay 2006), but the depth, multi- and trans-layered complexity, scope and scale of these conflicts need to be further studied, and linked to broader political economic discussions. A key methodological approach in doing this is to root the discussion to participant observations, thus avoiding the traps of using inadequate modern vocabularies to describe much more complex conflicts and their existential dimensions.

There are many types of extractivisms, ranging from agroextractivist monocultures to mineral extraction and hyper-extraction of freshwater sources, hydrocarbons, and energy, as well as forestry and new global value webs composed of food-feed-fiber-fuel complexes. I have reviewed and studied these different politics and sectors of extraction in relation to each other. In this book, I will draw on a variety of sectors, but taking into account the differences of distinct extractivist sectors and subsectors, whose differences should not be downplayed or conflated into an overall analysis of extractivism as a similar kind of opaque and amorphous process, which has happened with some users of the word and concept of capitalism. My key empirical focus is how different sectors affect forests. I aim to push the fields of thinking and practice related to deforestation to reconsider deforestations as redistributions of existences. Some, in fact most beings, both in numbers and variety terms, lose their lives, or their possibilities to continue to exist in the way they did once an area has been deforested.

I have looked at extractive projects with many different focuses, including tree plantations, monoculture plantations (soybean, corn, and cotton), ranching pastures, dam sites, and mining areas. These extractive projects have differing impacts on existences depending on the style and pace of extraction, and also the context. What is lost varies depending on the context, and this also includes the other-than-human beings, whose distribution varies. This has been noted for example by scholars of animism that compare highland and lowland Peru, who note that "nonhuman life in the lowlands has long been explored as animals and trees and in the highlands as infused within the mountains, the lakes, and the land" (Penfield 2019, 83). To understand these issues from the perspective of locals and how it feels in these localities, I visited the sites destroyed or targeted, and interviewed hundreds of social actors in key positions, mostly at the sites of destruction or at offices where decisions are made, e.g., company personnel, activists, local leaders, bureaucrats, and politicians, some of which are quoted in this book.

The theoretical insights presented in this book are also based on my participant observation at major deforestation sites (principally in the Brazilian states of Pará, Acre, Maranhão, Bahia, and Mato Grosso, and also in Peru's Madre de Dios province), wherein plantation expansion, mining ventures and other forms of extractivisms are taking place. This field research involved years of multi-sited political ethnography on the processes of different economic sectors' expansion in rural and forest areas, and particularly an observation of the politics and conflicts related to these moves in multiple-use conservation areas. For example, during November–December 2019, I did a field research trip to the Cerrado and Amazon traveling with a Finnish TV reporter for the National Broadcasting company YLE, their fixer, and a driver. The costs were shared and both of us made interviews with the same people. We traveled together from Cuiabá to Santarém in a van, as this was a dangerous path to roam alone, and doing field research there was expensive and much easier in a group. The journalist, Mika, normally first asked the questions, which the fixer or I then translated into Portuguese. Before and after this over 2,500-kilometer journey, I did individual field research.

For much of this book, I will focus on forests and trees, and will try to unite the existing political economic and ontological discussions with individual experiences. The book is also based on my own personal experiences. In the current setting of Finnish forest policy, it is legal for a private forest owner to clear-cut old-growth forests. For me, living in the countryside in Finland, next to farmers who have just in the past years deforested large areas of ancient forests, this state of affairs seems odd. In a city, one can have more decision-power through municipal governments and zoning over whether old forests are ravaged by developmental projects or not, but in the countryside, there is less democracy in this sense. The strict rules of private property give tenure rights to landholders to do as they please with the forests. If these farmers feel like they want to turn the forest into money, they can without outside intervention. They might even consider that clear-cutting would actually be an act of caring for the forest, which also may lead them to cut away the trees. Deforestation is typically followed by the establishment of tree plantations of one or at most a few species, typically spruce and pine. Much is lost in the conversion from forests into tree plantations. The amount and variety of different living beings is no longer found in the deforested area. Their existence has been extinguished. I feel that it is morally questionable that one person can have the power to decide upon the lives of so many other beings, and also on behalf of all other humans who might like to enjoy the forests and their berries, mushrooms, silence, trees, herbs, and everything else; including, their mere presence, closeness, and existence. However, these existential questions are absent in most of the current debates.

## The existential conflicts of extractivisms: Learning from Peru's Shipibo-Konibo

On the ground, the ontological conflicts of extractivisms are highly visible for example in mining and in other conflicts in the forests, where Indigenous and other traditional forest- and river-dwelling populations are pressured by the expansion of extractivisms. I encountered this kind of conflict when doing field research in Peru's Madre de Dios province in 2017, along the river with the same name. I was one of the first outside researchers to gain access to and travel with the Shipibo-Konibo Indigenous people of the Tres Islas community upriver, as they wanted to show me the illegal gold mining that was destroying their river, forests, and lakes.[6] At the same time, I was the first visitor on a planned tourist route they were piloting. We could travel there peacefully, although the air was very tense, as the boats we were taking were from the Indigenous community, and were known to the miners, who were armed. The navy had made surprise attacks and was destroying and burning mining equipment, there was a violent conflict in the region, and outsiders traveling to the area without locals would have been dangerous.

The interviews I conducted with the people in the community were done in-situ, we walked in the forest and rode in the river boats while I asked them about the impact of the issues above. The below excerpts illustrate how the locals tied extractivist activities to a whole set of offerings given by miners to spirits, so that they could do the mining, and how others saw that doing mining would hurt what some would call "spirits," which were there to protect the places. These were the key dynamics about the conflict that were offered to me. I was not given some materialist account of compensations or such modern politics.

> We believe, it is our belief, that miners are evil. They come here and scare the spirits of the forest, you know, the guardians of the forest. Unfortunately, they are evil miners, who come here, who come into this forest, and what they do is scare away the spirits of our forest—But, once in a while the spirits respond, right? Because there are times, you know, that they—mining is dangerous with a load, mining is dangerous. They work inside a hole, and we would like mother earth, as they say, to kill them for doing this. Even the miners are afraid of that. That is why they make a land payment, as they say, to appease the land, so that nothing will happen to them.

An interesting facet of this encounter of extractivism and Indigenous understandings is that even the miners, most of whom come from Cusco and Puno, and are highlands Andean Indigenous people or peasants themselves, also seem to live in an at least partially non-modernist world, as they also try to have reciprocal relations with Pachamama (the "World Mother" in Aymara and Quechua languages, one of the names of an Inca goddess), while destroying it:

> They [the miners] make, what they call, a land payment. It is like an offering to the land. I give you this, and you let me work in peace, that (is what they do).—They offer things like bread, champagne or beers, to the land.

However, the relation has already changed, so that the ritual seems to be now mostly empty, a remnant, and fear of the dire consequences, retribution by spirits, has been mostly forgotten. My informants referred to local "souls, black shadows" which are invisible, and do not step on the ground, called *Tunchi*, who appear during the night, and can kill you if you are in their way, and do not move aside when you hear their sound. These are "evil *Tunchis,*" "spirits of bad persons or so. Or other things." The key thing here is that one has to be respectful and pay attention for the *Tunchis*, which the miners have forgotten, "The miners are no longer afraid of them, you know. They basically just work and don't care. What they care about is the gold. That's it. To have money."

However, the Tres Islas native community member who showed me around the Madre de Dios river and forests, argued that the current stance of the miners is erroneous, as they are hurt themselves by their actions of transgression. This is apparent from the below reply to my question if gold has some kind of spirit:

> Sure, like everything. It is not the gold, it is mother earth. It is the spirit of the earth. That is why there is so much death in mining. Yes, yes, there is a lot of death. They die crushed under their load, anything, anything, they suffocate, all kinds of things. That's why it is evil—always. Mining is evil. It is bad for us.

At this time during our walk, we arrived at a beautiful lake, which was close to the Madre de Dios rivers, which has been partly mined. I asked if there were spirits in that lake:

> What my mother, who, like I said, recently passed away, and grandmother, always said is that, yes, the lake has a spirit. Its mother is said to be an anaconda. Yes, it is an anaconda.... And when they used to live up there, they would hear a noise at night, like "terretumba, ooo, tumba," rumble like a tremor, it felt like a tremor, and it always sounded at this place. And that is why they, we, don't want it to dry up because then the mother will not come out, the anaconda is there.

He followed up that the lake has not dried out, because the anaconda is inside the lake. I asked if the snake does not let the lake be destroyed. "Yes, miners who bring rafts here have disappeared. All of a sudden, they disappear. And we believe there is something else, something else." I asked what it is called. "The snake? Well, we call it simply as an anaconda. The spirits of mother earth, the mother of the lake. We know him."

Now, that I was deep in the Amazon forest, and with people who had lived there their whole lives, I also wanted to ask what they thought about trees, about what they are. The below reply to my question if there are spirits or persons or such inside trees, can help to understand the care and non-utilitarian, life-respecting attitude that is an antidote to extractivism:

> Well, mostly in medicinal trees, right, they are, they have spirits, because there is medicine. There are trees, like I said,—for evil. That are good for that [for evil purposes]. Not only good, but also for evil. And this can harm you, that is what we believe. As I said, the *oje* is a good tree. But there is one—called *chichuachi* that cannot be cut by anybody. *Lupuna colorada*. You cannot cut that because it will be bad. If we knowingly cut it—yes, if we cut it knowing that it is bad - something bad will happen to us.—Our part where we urinate, we cannot urinate—an intense pain. That is why we cut these and those are not cut by just anyone. Only someone like this, a bijo, who knows how to tell the tree why it is being cut down, right? What it is being cut down for, with a reverence, and cuts it down. And then nothing happens.

I asked for further clarifications, and got the answer that the spirit of that particular tree is evil, and if the tree is killed, the spirit travels to another tree. Some trees are also good, and I asked if these trees help them. "Yes, they help…they communicate with us, we believe." I asked how the trees communicate, and received the following reply, which emphasized that the trees use humans as mediators, to communicate their message, and this is how they have noted this:

> They wanted, you know, to cut down a tree that you are not supposed (to cut down). We dreamt about it. You should not cut it, because it is like us, you know? By cutting this one you would be killing one of us.
>
> That is why we dream about this sometimes. A tree, its spirit still has a life to live, right, to grow and it does not want us to kill it.
>
> Now, if we are going to do it for a reason, you know, for something that we really need, we do it. We don't dream. Everything is normal—peaceful. It doesn't do anything to you, it doesn't "chog" [I did not understand this word] you. It doesn't do anything to you.—If I'm going to cut down a tree for—the tree tells me that it knows why I am going to cut it down, and I have even dreamt about it. My old man, my parents, you know? They have always taught us to do these things, you know?

> You never cut down a tree that you are not going to use. If you are going to use it, cut it down. If not, don't. Let it grow. It is like a human being who wants to live to an old age. Like any of us. That, you know, is our belief [about] everything.

At this point of the conversation, I wanted to return to the dream I had in 2005 on my first night in the Amazon. Even in the memory I could feel the panic and the anguish I felt in that dream (and upon waking), to discover the large trees were all cut down. I asked from my Indigenous guide, what such a dream signifies. He gave the reply below, while we walked next to the lake where about fifteen giant otters were said to live, which offers an excellent view into how many Indigenous people see the extractivist attitude and practices. I asked, "what does it mean, to have a dream where there are big trees, that have been cut down?" He responded with the following:

> It is grief. It is, it means grievance, suffering. You know? That they didn't want this—that they didn't want to die an early death. There are many who cut down the trees, they do, and it is bad for us. And they, sometimes, you tell of a dream, you know, of a very profound sadness when they come and cut down trees, you now? And this is felt.
>
> They, themselves, feel it. I, for one, feel it, as I said, you know? Look, when they cut down trees for mining here, one feels it, you know? Because it shouldn't be like this, the land does not want this, you know? It is that feeling—that spirit—that makes you dream.
>
> They send us a sign for us to stop this—this is destruction to the spirits, who are in pain.
>
> It is as if they cut your arm or your hand, it is a wound. Do you understand? A wound. If I cause a wound, that is sad, right? That would be bad, right? You wouldn't be happy.
>
> That is why we always dream, we are always told, enough with the mining. For them to leave us.—Do not allow a hole to be left as it is like a hole in my stomach. It means that they do not love the spirit.
>
> That is why we always come, we try, we fight those miners. We fight, but not with our fists, you know? We enforce our values, we stand up to them and throw them out. Gentlemen, leave! We don't want you here anymore.
>
> Because the spirit is great, here. That, and our spirits, too. There are spirits that are happy, because we are bringing people who will help us, for the first time. And there will be people like those

> who — and when they see the miners, it scares them, it startles them to see what they are doing here, you know?
>
> But they know that once a place is touristy, they won't be here or have any support. Why? Because it is bad, right? It gives a bad impression, right? This we know, right? But as you have seen, the lake is beautiful. It is beautiful to us because it is our heritage—left to us by our ancestors - and we want to care for it.
>
> We have seen that there are some young people who have done this recently. During a time that we left, right? These *moritos* [young people] will not go out, we didn't have these people before, who wanted to protect that, the lake.
>
> But now that we are, we are fighting.... We are already fighting [referring to our presence, at that moment, in the mining conflict area]. We are here to make a gathering as a group of people. We come, we throw them out, they leave. But, then, others come back. Others come back to work. That is the problem.
>
> And, like I said, we get almost no help from the government, you know? If they were to come, we are—staying where this happens now. We go there, we go to defend—we call the police.
>
> But there is no such help. Unfortunately, there isn't any, you know? That is our greatest sorrow, that they are putting an end to the spirit of our land.

This book illustrates via the above kind of direct quotes how extractivisms change worlds and how they are related to existences. I assess who wins and loses with extractivist expansion, and what power and existential redistributions this change entails.

To date, in the discussion of resource extractions the focus of political economy or ecology has been on relations of capital, labor, sociocultural dimensions, or other factors with the attention, especially, on the relations of control and power that the spatial territorializing at the core of the creation of commodity frontiers entails (Rasmussen and Lund 2018). Both Leftist and other political economies, as well as several political ecologies, typically do not seriously challenge the Cartesian dualism or modernity's scales of valuing life (Gudynas 2017), which may be one reason why the question of existences has not been a central issue. However, there is a need to understand that extractivist expansions are also processes of existential extinctions. They are maybe many more of these types of processes than anything else. Based on this approach, I propose the four questions below as the key questions for an existential scoping of agrarian political economy, critical agrarian studies, and other socioenvironmental studies.

They can be used for studying and complementing political economic and other analyses on different scales of environmental change, and assessing differing productive processes from the perspective of their impacts on existences:

1 Who or what exists?
2 How they can exist (what is the quality of existence)?
3 In which time and/or how long they exist?
4 Who are the key entities deciding and contesting the rights to exist?

These are important questions, and open up what I mean by the redistribution of existences. The discussion needs to go beyond the current anthropocentric approach, where existences, if even mentioned, refer solely to humans (e.g., Rasmussen and Lund 2018).[7] By existences, I refer to human and other-than-human existences of beings and species, thus re-framing, for example "biodiversity" as being constituted by multiple existences within a web and circle of life, and, in comparison, monoculture (plantations) being constituted by far fewer existences (species/beings).[8] The next chapters will open up these issues and the four questions in detail, and they will be used as key questions throughout the chapters of this book.

I will first review the most recent research on extractivisms, and note how it has and has not taken into account existential redistributions and extinctions. Chapter 1 will identify several new publications that are rapidly starting to change different fields of scholarship, through an approach that is partially similar to the approach taken in this book. Chapter 2 discusses what a political economy of existences should entail. It opens up in detail the way extractivisms of different types should be characterized, and operationalized for research. I identify different degrees of extractivisms, and offer examples from different sectors, including a comparison with non extractivist activities. These comparisons are based on my own field research on different extractive sectors, including open-pit iron ore and gold mining, forestry operations of different kinds, ranching, agribusiness plantations of different kinds, and agroforestry and agroecological farming, conducted by different social groups in different parts of the world. Chapter 3 continues from the theoretical and empirical comparisons of existential political economy presented in the prior chapters, offering a practical example of how to apply the four key questions identified above. I do this through a detailed discussion of northern Mato Grosso's soybean plantations deforesting expansion over the Cerrado and

Amazon forests, which used to be inhabited by Indigenous peoples and countless other-than-humans. I offer notes, especially, on the soybean-livestock production complex, but also on many other things, such as the rapid deployment of mechanized and automated operations where human laborers are hardly needed, reflecting on what these extractivist intensifications mean in terms of existences and extinctions. I draw on more classical political economic analysis, as well as on the above kind of political ontological reflections on what has changed, how, in what time, and by which actors, when forests are erased to make way for agroextractivism. After this, the concluding chapter unites the prior discussions, and links these developments at the point of extraction to the global cascade of existential impacts within the soybean chain. The conclusions will also discuss extractivisms and existences and their links to the past, ongoing, and foreseen world-systemic and world-ecological transformations, making reflections on the Plantationocene (Haraway 2016; Wolford 2021), Capitalocene (Moore 2016), and the Anthropocene as designations given to the currently unfolding era. I reflect how the lessons in this book may help in addressing these broader discussions, and identify some future directions for both research and transformative alternatives to extractivisms.

## Notes

1. Different scholars use the listed concepts to refer to other-than human (ways of) being. More-than-human is preferred by Political Ontology (de la Cadena and Blaser 2018) as well as many Amazonian anthropologists, as non-human is not as accurate in many instances. For example, among Amazon Indigenous populations, people can be at the same time jaguars, human, and something in-between, called a were-jaguar (see Kohn 2013). Trans-modernity is discussed by Grosfoguel (2011), as a process where traditionality or indigeneity continues, but is translated for modern purposes (see also de la Cadena 2015 for these political practices). Indigenous people can for example adapt to modern technologies for their own purposes, in a transmodern process. This does not mean that they would be automatically "corrupted," but in fact, modern tools and even ontologies are strategically used by many Indigenous people in decolonial struggles and processes.
2. Oxum is one of the principal divinities in the Afro-Brazilian Umbanda and other religions. She helps and guides the humanity to live on this planet, and also takes the human form, breastfeeding a baby by a riverside, which represents all her beauty and kindness, her sources of power. She reigns especially over non-salty, fresh waters. She can simultaneously take the form of a river and a woman.
3. In the Brazilian context, "traditional populations" refers to the rural populations that have lived for a long time in particular places and have developed identities based on particular livelihoods that are rooted in

those places (such as rubber tapper, riverside dweller, artisanal fisher, nut collector, and so on). It should be mentioned that in Portuguese many of these populations are called extractivist populations; however, this use of the term should not be confused with the negative connotations associated with the Spanish and English term extractivism. These populations, at least partially, share similar non-modernist understandings of their territories as the Indigenous groups and the Afro-Brazilian communities described above (see Kröger and Lalander 2016).

4. Viveiros de Castro (2012) explains in his study of cosmological perspectivism that Amazonian systems of thought are not part of a multiculturalism but of multinaturalism. Multiculturalism entails relativism and refers to "the same and common nature or reality, regarded by different cultural points of view," while multinaturalism entails perspectivism, and refers to "different corporeal states that presupposes a similar human and cultural condition" (Vanzolini and Cesarino 2014, 1). Other-than-human actors should not be understood as a cultural feat, in a relativistic sense; such ontologies should also not be seen as something that just Indigenous people "have" in the same manner as they would have a distinct "culture" (de la Cadena 2015). Indigenous movements propose different politics and key actors, including other-than-humans, these exceeding the current notions of political (e.g., in multiculturalism's concepts of "gender, race, ethnicity, or sex," as argued by Micarelli and Verran (2018, 124). The onto-epistemologies within these spheres are plural not because of those human-divisions, but because the actors include also other-than-humans in the political arena (de la Cadena 2010).
5. The notes below on *väki* are based on several sources, such as museum displays in Finnish forest museums, discussions with people knowledgeable about the old uses of this concept, as well as the following books, among others, from which one can read folkloric analyses (see Siikala 1992; Talve 1990). The naming of different non-modern entities and beings varied across the different regions of what is today Finland, and the same entity, such as an elf or spirit, could have many names.
6. See http://www.datoindigena.pe/#/madre-de-dios/comunidad/3 for basic information on the Tres Islas community and their conflicts.
7. Here some examples from the article on frontiers by Rasmussen and Lund (2018, 396), which highlight the anthropocentrism of analysis, which is in dire contrast with South American Political Ontology, for example, "such negative potentialities condition the territorializations and threaten not only to eliminate human bodies, but also to erase cultural ideas and values." And, "humans make frontiers and territories, and the symbolic and real erasures are accompanied by representations of what is, and what is desired, in maps, histories, political projects, and, not least, commodities."
8. In contrast and addendum to the concepts of resource or commodity frontier, the site of transforming existing ontologies, sites where rights and practices of existence are remade as beings/species change their relations to resource extraction, I propose to use the concept of "frontier of existence."

# 1 Extractivisms, existences, and extinctions

New studies on existences and extractivism have emerged in the past few years. In particular, Indigenous scholars and scholarship have started to ask more vocally for a broadening of understandings. This means that the prior analyses focusing on neo-extractivist economic-social projects and their role in defining the country strategies in Latin America in the 2000s need to be better united with other understandings, including different theoretical, global, and broad analyses of the existential facets behind extractivist attitudes and practices.

A key reason for writing this book stems from the skewed and blind modern and Western ways of understanding and observing lived environments that are often mechanistic and reductionist. This way of viewing the world often means that not all destruction is seen or recognized. This means that most lost individuals, species, connections, and relations are left out of the proverbial report. The existing entanglements and their destruction are not noted, and other kinds of existences are ignored or simply not understood. This lack of acknowledgement or understanding does not mean that these existences are not there, but they remain in the shadows. Thus, putting existences into the limelight of the debates around extractivisms serves to emphasize *how much* destruction, death, and disintegration extractivisms actually cause. This pit is even deeper than one could think, and the depth of this destruction is not emphasized enough, even within the extractivism scholarship that focuses on political economic analysis. Yet, there is also an increase in calls for more attention and recognition to be given to existences, as the absence of these are seen as pivotal for the whole process of how and why extractivisms can continue to exist and expand, despite their violence. For example, Leifsen (2020) argues that this mode of non-recognition is essential for extractivism, not only by allowing the erasure and incorporation of all that is not recognized but also in delimiting what could constitute

DOI: 10.4324/9781003102977-2

something which could even be compensated. This limits the understanding of what is considered valuable or even existing, and makes it more understandable how even so-called progressive governments have embraced neo-extractivism, on the hope that this model could be used for social policy funding.

I want to emphasize here that my intention is not to downplay or chastise the existing political economic analyses of extractivism, but instead to complement them. The "extraordinary profitability and extreme poverty" that extractivist projects create (Svampa 2019, 7), and on which they are premised, should never be forgotten. Current global extractivism is, at its core, a continuation of the neoliberal process. Neoliberalism, as viewed through Harvey's (2005) neomarxist understanding, is primarily a project designed to restore the class inequalities and exorbitant elite wealth that were curbed during the era of the New Deal and other post-World War II redistributive social reforms. Extractivism is an extremely effective way to ensure elite wealth and can permanently lock others out from possibilities for capital accumulation, since productive lands, as a key form of capital, are refashioned through a politics of lock-in (e.g., open-pit mines and poisoned plantations) to serve only the large extractivist operations and interests. This process gained significant momentum during the 1990s, when mining exploration increased by 2,000 percent in South America, and 90 percent globally (Rivera Andía and Ødegaard 2019). The scale and scope of extractivist projects have only continued to accelerate since. This parallels the massive losses in lives, wherein biologists underline the magnitude of current "extinction crises at both [the] species and population levels" and "extinction cascades, [which are] a series of extinctions triggered by the disappearance of a keystone species in an ecosystem" (Ceballos et al. 2020, 13600). Relatively, when comparing all the world's regions, these losses have been by far the worst in Latin America and the Caribbean, where there has been an astounding 94 percent average loss in the non-human population since 1970 (WWF 2020). It is no wonder that the extractivisms and Political Ontology scholarship (de la Cadena and Blaser 2018), the study of eco-territorial movements (Porto-Gonçalves 2006), and the biocentric turn (Gudynas 2009) either started or have deep roots in Latin America. This is a reason why I focus on South America in this book, since in this region, the dynamics of contemporary extractivisms and extinctions are most urgently present.

Global extractivism presents an even more destructive continuation of neoliberalism, taking form by the widening of financial portfolios to include to a greater degree those corporations that extract "natural resources" and "raw materials." Many important Wall Street funds have called for this expansion of investor portfolios, including GMO, whose key owner, Jeremy Grantham, in 2011 characterized the rapid rise, which started in 2005, of commodity values in relation to capital goods in historical world markets, as a new "commodity paradigm" (Blodget 2011). It should be noted that later, in 2016, Grantham went against his prior prediction and argued that much of the commodity price rise had been a normal bubble (Bryan 2016). However, I think it is still too early to throw away the commodity paradigm hypothesis. One needs to have a longer perspective when observing the rises and falls in natural resource-related politics, such as deforestation rates, whose short-term fluctuations are systematically taken as signs of supposedly continuing tendencies (Kröger and Nygren 2020). The relative downfall of commodity prices in the 2014–2018 period is now over. If you look at the prices of traded "commodities" other than the energy-related ones, such as gold, lumber, beef, poultry, soybeans, or iron ore,[1] or the stocks of the corporations profiting from these commodities, they have not come down substantially or returned to their pre-2005 levels. In fact, their prices have soared to a record high since the COVID-19 pandemic. This rise is not only related to the pandemic but also to the cascading climate and socio-ecological crises and is on par with the increasing resistance efforts, which have rendered several would-be extraction sites outside the bounds of politically feasible extraction expansion, from the Arctic to India and Brazil (Kröger 2019a, 2020a). The 2008 financial crisis further advanced this crisis of capitalism, which needs to find new frontiers of extraction to feed new inputs into the circuits and processes of capital accumulation (Moore 2015). Land, resource, and control grabbing were central elements of this phenomenon (Borras et al. 2011, 2012; White et al. 2012), offering greater access for extractivist projects to take hold of the territories grabbed.

One could say that the essential point about global extractivism is that it can only continue to last for a short while before planetary collapses change the situation so that even those who still accrue gains from extractivism join the mass of sufferers. In fact, this is already happening, as shown by examples like the 2020 fires in Australia and the extreme cold weather event in Texas in February 2021. These events also affected the people who made the decisions to further expand coal mines and oil extraction operations in their home regions. Biological studies suggest that we are currently living through the sixth mass extinction where "many of the species that have been driven to the brink will likely become extinct soon," which, when considering humans, "may be the most serious environmental threat to the persistence of civilization, because it is irreversible" (Ceballos et al. 2020, 13596).

The analyses of value and capital formation, accumulation processes, and existential redistributions, need to be merged. Under the current situation, no sound analysis of international relations (IR) or other politics can shy away from considering the magnitude of the ecological crises. In fact, this type of change has already started to take place in the IR scholarship, but there is still much that needs to be done (Kröger 2020b). Analyzing extractivist projects can open a window to see how existence depends on profit-making calculations and practices. These practices have already caused extractivist violences for several centuries (Gudynas 2015) in the key spots and moments where the capitalist world-ecology has expanded. An example of this occurred when global tar capitalism targeted the Finnish forests in the nineteenth century, turning existing swidden commons into tar. Toivanen and Kröger (2019) emphasize that the key mechanisms through which such capitalist world-ecologies are expanded include death, debt, and dispossession. Capital accumulation, and the links of these economic changes to the ecology, livelihoods, access to land, and the right to live, need to be merged in analyses of political economy and political ecology. Grosfoguel (2016) argues that the Western human-nature dichotomy, in which the idea of owning nature is a key mechanism, separates human individuals from their community, and humans from their places of existence and subsistence.

Yet, this is not where the story ends. I wish to provide a more sensitive analysis called for by Leifsen (2020, 9) to challenge the "highly restricted understanding of the intervened reality" on which extractivist incorporations of places are based. The discussion around extractivist projects herein is related to what kind of *politics*, in a broader sense, are allowed. I think it is better to talk of projects, to emphasize the different and piecemeal ways in which the destruction takes place, and not to reify some sort of abstract idea of this process. Extractivists would like to retain and deepen the politics-as-usual of Western modernity's valuations, while their resistance—particularly those aspects that have been successful—is trying to usher in a new kind of politics (or, actually, a mix of new and old), where non- or trans-modernist framings are used, sometimes causing transformations at the metapolitical level, and gaining victories partially through those metapolitics (see de la Cadena 2015; Gudynas 2015; Kröger 2020a).

## Existences in the extractivism scholarship

Looking at the most recent literature on extractivism, it can be argued that this research is not inherently borne to consider or analyze existences, or other-than-human beings (such as animals). Instead, the focus of the following publications has been on extractivism as a contentious and conflictive economic/political action or phenomenon (e.g., Engels 2021), on global extractivist and logistical circuits and political economy (e.g., Arboleda 2020), on juxtaposing extractivism with human or citizen rights (e.g., Hougaard and Vélez-Torres 2020), or on social movements (e.g., Lyra 2019). A common thread is the recognition of sacrifice zones, ecological damage, and economic inequality in extractivism (e.g., Gomez-Pereira 2020; Healy et al. 2019); yet, what is being destroyed is rarely discussed in detail or elaborated upon. The focus of many studies is still decidedly anthropocentric, and in fact, often limited to humans. This is the case even in some of the gendered and intersectional critiques of extractivism, such as in the special issue of *Human Geography*, edited by Caretta and Zaragocin (2020), where the focus is on women's daily embodied experiences of water, rather than a further broadening of the scope of whose existences are considered (with the one exception of Astrid Ulloa's (2020) article on relational water justice). In many studies of extractivism, the leap toward more inclusive and relational ontological vocabularies is not taken. The existences or living beings subject to the extraction are not discussed in favor of concepts, such as landscape, ecosystem, nature, natural resource, and biodiversity to refer to the mass of non-humans (e.g., Arboleda 2020; Healy et al. 2019; Riofrancos 2020). This is the case also in Ye et al. (2020); however, this exploration does emphasize that extractivism results in barrenness and void, which could be understood as referring to extinction, at least when talking about what exists. This barrenness may refer to an emptying of some mass or material; yet, as I argue here, not only voids are created, as there are also some new existences created, globally, in a cascading manner. However, these interventions of extractivism in the web of life can be quite short-lived and can lead—in a matter of decades—to the kind of barrenness that is described as a key characteristic of extractivism—even in several of the above analyses.

There is a need to challenge the commonly used vocabulary and analytics of "resources" and "commodities," and even of notions such as "bio"-whatever, "ecology," and "economy," to the extent that these do not consider that they are discussing and trying to depict a living world. Even if the focus is on calculating masses or abstract units, this also has political ontological impacts. De la Cadena and Blaser (2018) warn the danger of treating the non-modernist understandings of the more-than-human natures as beings in their own right, as if these were just an understanding that is held by Indigenous peoples. "Nature's rights" should not be seen as only a matter of concern to some human groups, or as a cultural feat. This way of framing these debates seems to be adopted in some strands of the literature, e.g., in

Riofrancos (2020), which provides an otherwise important discussion on how a broader anti-extractivism in Ecuador has led to discussions on granting value and agency to other-than-human existences. Also, Scott (2020), while briefly mentioning Indigenous peoples' cosmologies as a contrast to extractivism, seems to treat such understandings as something that Indigenous people have, instead of taking a Political Ontological approach, which would be more attuned to scope extractivisms and existences.

The recent scholarship on extractivisms has different strands and takes, and this book contributes to these discussions through a much needed focus on existences. There is still a lot of scholarship on the politics of extraction that is conducted utilizing the vocabularies-as-usual (e.g., the volume of meat produced), or without including the analysis of more-than-human actors. Often this choice is made for disciplinary conventions, to bring a focus to the piece, or for publishing reasons, rather than trying to consciously downplay or deny the complexities involved. For example, Bebbington et al. (2018) mention that they are aware of the Andean Political Ontology literature, yet decide to use different vocabularies. However, it is ever more important to change vocabularies and give more credit and attention to the actual lives visibly at stake (including those possibly or even invisibly at stake, beyond the cognition Western modernity), given the rapid shift in consciousness regarding the destruction of lives in broader sense. This shift is gaining pace even as I write these words. However, there is a simultaneous backlash, as the extractivist expansions have led to a rise of authoritarianisms across the political scale, which is visible across Latin America. Worryingly, there are also attempts by leftist politicians and scholars, who frame themselves as class fighters, to delegitimize the *buen vivir* and other similar post-extractivist advocates and Indigenous rights supporters by implying that they work for imperialist neoliberal projects. These schisms have only increased during COVID-19, e.g., in Peru and Bolivia (Signatories 2021). Gudynas (2020b) refers to such Marxist class thinking as being a part of modernity and operating under its developmentalist logic.

It is not only the broader field of studying "natural resources" or the politics of extraction (Kröger 2020b, 2020c), where existential considerations are far fewer than in the study of extractivisms, that need to be complemented by a greater consideration and inclusion of existences, but also the scholarship on extractivisms. Even some pioneers of extractivism scholarship have taken approaches that focus mostly on political economy in developmental or political terms. For example, *The New Extractivism* by Veltmeyer and Petras (2014) is a Marxist assessment of the imperialist character of new commodity-export focused economic policies of especially Latin American governments. In another example, Acosta (2017) emphasizes the creation of social inequality as the key problem, consequence, and driving mechanism of extractivism. The focus of this work is not on other-than-human beings or existences in a broader sense. Furthermore, Acosta (2017) argues that the way toward post-extractivism is the wider distribution of extractivist gains, after which a transition would start to non-extractivist activities. However, in my view, this is questionable, given the trajectories of Latin American neo-extractivist experimentations since the 2000s. The political landscape was changed so that after the state-boosted consolidation of power to large extractivist corporations, there were fewer political possibilities to revert the power of landholding elites (Andrade 2020; Kröger 2012). Acosta (2017) portrays getting rid of the global inequality and dependence on continued and destructive raw material exports as the key to overcome extractivism. Instead, there should be a focus on regional and national autonomy through a strategic use of export revenues. However, this was exactly the approach adopted, e.g., by Bolivia and Venezuela, yet they did not manage to overturn capitalism or dependency, and the impacts on the environment were extremely harmful, and caused violent socio-political conflict (Ranta 2018; SOSOrinoco 2021). A further problem of the kind of "practical" thinking represented in Acosta (2017) (however, it should be noted that in some other publications there are different takes) is the consideration of points of extraction as non-unique, and the treatment of *buen vivir*, *sumak kawsay*, and *suma qamaña* as utopian thoughts and plans, instead of analyzing how these cosmovisions and lifeworlds are already being lived in the here and now of the real world. In other words, there are already many post-extractivist worlds existing in the world, and the contention that they can exist is not simply a utopian dream.

Differing from the publications discussed above, this book provides a detailed contribution on existential redistributions, ontological conflicts, and world-ecological and regional transformations based on in-depth and long-term field research and multi-sited political ethnography. The focus is on the ideological, cosmological, and existential dimensions inherent in extractivist expansions, not only on the macro-economic policies and government projects of neo-extractivism. This book is global and transdisciplinary in character, in contrast to the bulk of existing books, which are more focused on particular theoretical schools (such as anthropological and sociological discussions, or particular Marxist theoretical schools), or do not connect the regionally situated dynamics to their world-ecological consequences. Furthermore, new books are urgently needed for creating suitable theoretical frameworks and prognoses of the post-COVID-19 world. This book will provide new organizing concepts and a theoretical framework for starting to analyze the unfolding environmental politics of the post-COVID-19, climate emergency, and ever-more chaotic, multipolar world.

Besides the above examples of literature focusing more on political economy or not emphasizing existences, there are studies that do consider existences to varying degrees and in differing ways. Next, I will assess a selection of these studies in more detail.

*Indigenous Women and Climate Change*, edited by Silva-Santisteban (2020), contains several important chapters discussing extractivism. In this volume, Acosta (2020, 16), building on Gudynas (2013), makes the important point that violating "human and natural rights" is a necessary condition for extractivism to exist. The chapter by de la Cadena (2020) offers an important critique for understanding the fallacies of the widely used compensation policies and applications. The key here is that extractivist projects cannot compensate for what is lost, since the losses are unique, and tied to lives of locals, which are embedded in particular places (see Ehrnström-Fuentes 2020). This work uses a Peruvian mining conflict as an example. The mine would destroy particular Andean lagoons, against the promise of giving access to water from a different source. Using this "tradeoff" de la Cadena (2020, 40) exemplifies how this is not an option for the locals because "the lagoons are their life: their plants, animals, soils, trees, families are with that specific water which cannot be translated into water from reservoirs, not even if, as the mining corporation promises, they would provide more water." Lassila (2020) offers a similar critique based on Arctic mining cases, extending the critique of compensation schemes to include the currently developing policies of "ecological compensation," whereby a company argues they would find an equal place without ore that they would protect if they are allowed to mine and destroy another protected area with ore. These policies of ecological compensation have even been supported by environmentalists and biologists, who see great potential for this route if it is endorsed by laws that ensure at least some protection from extractivist activities somewhere. Yet, such ecological-biological thinking is not aware of, or does not take into account, the ontological complexities and violence involved in the process.

Leifsen (2020) contributes to this discussion of compensation through an article that makes excellent points around the concept that I will call the redistributions of existences. Extractivist projects, such as mines, seldom manage to wipe out everything. Instead, these projects are placed on top of existing relations. As Leifsen (2020, 1) expresses, "rather we see the assemblage of a new mining reality that is superimposed on other forms of life." Thus, it depends not only on the type of extractivism (e.g., an open-pit or underground mine) but also on the context, and the prior assemblages and entanglements of the context. This includes what kind of redistributions of existences and potentially related ontological and other conflicts that are prone to emerge in that context. Extractivisms are also processes that operate through and end up creating new kinds of existences, by particular mechanisms, which typically differ in their mechanistic homogenization drive from the heterogenous diversity of non extractivisms. Leifsen (2020) describes how mining projects create new kinds of settings, thereby reducing the material complexity by separating minerals from other substances. This reduction of material complexity is extremely important for extractivism to be able to scale up via global markets. These kinds of processes are essential for understanding how extractivisms become global extractivisms, which can also be translated into the reduction of complexities, and the killing and reduction of diversity and relations of life. The mechanisms of cloning, scaling up, and mechanization are essential in the process of global extractivist redistributions of existences. These result in the destruction of places, which are replaced by wasted, barren, or toxic areas.

Violence is a key component of extractivisms. In Latin America, India, and many parts of Africa and Asia, as well as also in the parts of the Global North, which could be called pockets of "Global South" (such as Indigenous areas violated by extractivisms in North America and the Arctic), this also means dire physical violence against local populations and in general the people who try to actively defend these places. For example, Svampa (2019) notes the extractive violence against people and communities resisting the extractivist projects of governments, corporations, or paramilitaries in Latin America (however, she does not emphasize or discuss extractivism as an overall violence in the web of life, against both humans and other-than-humans). Navarro Trujillo (2020) opens up extractivist processes as offensives that carry an existential threat for re-producing life in all its forms. Polo Blanco and Piñeiro Aguiar (2019) argue that the torture of the planet by an extractivism-led global capitalism creates wasted lives, human waste, underdogs, and forgotten people, who may serve as cheap labor. For the more-than-humans, this translates as a typical destiny of depletion, abandonment, and being turned into waste. This resonates with the conceptualization of an ever-larger portion of humanity as surplus population, who are simply not needed anymore for direct capital accumulation in the neoliberal era (Li 2010). However, this is not just a story of dispossession, or not having jobs for all, but, a much deeper process of imposing the Western understanding that land and living beings can be (dis)possessed—in fact, in their own terms, some Indigenous and other people were and are not dispossessed if (and when) they see that they belong to the land rather than that the land would belong to them (Nichols 2020). This was especially the case with Amerindians during the 500 years of conquest of the Americas.

There is a far-reaching "contemporary colonial ontological occupation of territories" that is not limited only to extractivism, but makes absent all kinds of worlds that make different places (de la Cadena and Blaser 2018, 3). According to Milanez (2019, 128), for the Yanomani-Shaman Davi Kopenawa, this "disturbance in ontological relationships" causes a state of illness and imbalance called *xawara*. This illness is spread particularly amongst the Indigenous and rural peasant communities, who are already in a downtrodden position, in multiple ways. *Indigenous Peoples, Extractivism, and Turbulences in South America*, edited by Rivera Andía and Ødegaard (2019, 30), and drawing on Escobar (2016) notes that Indigenous life projects in the Americas are being increasingly "troubled, subdued, ignored," framed and fabricated as not existing by extractivist project proponents. Life and lives are thus emphasized in this innovative book. Stensrud (2019, 145–146) distinguishes "extractivist" projects as an opposite to "life-making projects." Importantly, she also notes that these can be very much entangled in practice, some miners participating in both, e.g., by sharing the ontological world where earth-beings are to be considered and pleased. However, at the end Stensrud (2019, 146) underlines that "a logic based on extractivism and conquest is not compatible with the logic of relationality and reciprocity," this being an important finding considering the plethora of interventions trying to regulate or formalize activities like illegal mining (studied, e.g., in Zabyelina and van Uhm (2020)). In line with this, Guzmán-Gallegos (2019) emphasizes how extraction sites are also sites of extinction. I want to draw more attention to this point about extinction rather than the possibilities of the various forms of capital accumulation.

These existential threats of extractivism also explain the particular kind of resistance that extractivist projects have faced. Ehrnström-Fuentes (2020) argues that the collective threat of death and the will to live explain a great deal of the new extractivist conflicts, where territorial, place-based social movements of Indigenous and peasant populations affect mobilization and territories. *ExtrACTION* by

Jalbert et al. (2017) analyzes some of the globally most prolific extractivist conflicts, such as the resistance to new oil pipelines in North America. The strategies by which resistance to forestry and mining extractivism are most likely to succeed are studied in Kröger (2013a, 2020a). Milanez (2019) approaches the quality of this resistance, this defense of alternative life-projects and territorial difference in the face of ecocidal/genocidal extractivism as "re-existence," thus making an important contribution to the understanding of what is currently at stake. Milanez (2019, 126) argues that the militaristic extractivism of the Bolsonaro regime in Brazil includes "racial extermination" and torture. This extractivism is based on the idea that the Amazon would be akin to an empty planet, where history only starts, and the place only becomes real when extractivist corporations arrive. There are multiple dimensions to the violence of this extractivism, such as draining away "the substance of the past" and imposing "a daily routine of suffering, the *xawara* described by Yanomani," which "destroys the perspective of a future" (Milanez 2019, 129). This note on the perspective of a future is especially important, and I will return to it in the next chapter, when discussing the four key questions for existential political economy in more detail.

The many forms and paces that extractive violence can take and which dominate the overall contemporary logic at the planetary scale are opened up in the chapters of *Our Extractive Age*, edited by Shapiro and McNeish (2021). Therein, the logic and violence caused by extractivism is also expanded from the more directly tangible "natural resource" analysis to the digital, data, and virtual realms (Chagnon, Hagolani-Albov, and Hokkanen 2021), which indeed are closely intertwined, dependent upon, or feeding the more readily visible extractivisms that directly destroy habitable environments. These realms and how existences are redistributed within them through their transformations—whether separately or more tightly in connection with changes in the more readily tangible world—is an area that needs more study, e.g., based on the application of the four key questions identified in this book. The etymological roots of extractivism are also addressed in *Our Extractive Age*. By this, extractivisms are referred to as an inherently violent process of pulling something out by force in such a way that radically transforms the existing order (Durante, Kröger, and LaFleur 2021). These etymological roots are considered alongside many other contributions on the violence of contemporary extractivisms. Similarly, Dunlap and Jakobsen's (2020) *Violent Technologies of Extraction* significantly augments the sphere of economic activities and investment projects which should be considered as violent (for both human and "non-human persons"). Dunlap (2020) further draws on Huseman and Short's (2012, 216) concept of "slow industrial genocide" to refer to what is being done now against the earth and its populations. Of course, for those locals who have had first-hand experiences of being massacred within the extractivist expansions, these changes are not slow (Broad 2021). Yet, these shifts are mostly made invisible and distant to those not experiencing them personally (Ioris 2017). This results in a sensation of a slow pace and rhythm of destruction, which is hard to spot. For example, climate and ecological catastrophes are difficult to identify or intervene on, as these are "cumulative sociomaterial changes" which "lose their eventfulness over time," as Ollinaho (2016, 53) importantly notes. This is particularly the case in the Global North, wherein the everyday lives of people are mostly disconnected from the actual realities and violence in the places where extractivist projects are expanded, which are mostly located in the Global South, or under regimes of greater compensation that ameliorate the trade-offs perceived by a group of key local social actors in the Global North. More broadly, for those living the lifestyle associated with the North, mostly as passive consumer-citizens, the violences are irrelevant news, as "environmental changes are imposed to the consciousness as intellectual problems, which tend to be incommensurate with the pragmatic necessities of everyday life" (Ollinaho 2016, 53). Dunlap (2020) makes a linked observation about how not only wars but also the so-called peacetimes are not peaceful at all, as industrial developmental regimes naturalize the erasure of what I call existences. These points merit much more study. There should especially be further study of the insightful (de)linking of the Global North from the extractivisms of the Global South, following the framework provided by Ollinaho (2016). This should go beyond noting that there are ecologically unequal trade relations, ecological debt, and uneven development between the North and the South, as the metabolic rift, ecological economics, and environmental justice literatures have studied at length (Bunker 1985; Foster 1999; Hornborg 2011; Martinez-Alier 2002; Saes and Bisht 2020). Moore (2017) argues that it is essential to dissolve the boundaries of environment and society in future analysis of metabolic rifts and shifts, and give greater attention to extra-human natures. There must be greater attention paid to existences in all their diversity and multiple relations, also when conducting political economic analysis. There is an especially dire need for identifying and supporting transformative alternatives to the current violent state of the world.

Extractivism literature has also analyzed how extractivist projects change socio-economic-cultural relations. Eufemia et al. (2019, 2) use an analysis of Columbia to explain how the delicate balance and relations of local communities and identities are transformed, as there is "an intrinsic link between the depletion of natural resources and the erosion of local cultures." The impacts of extractive interventions are multifold and take place on many interconnected levels. Eufemia et al. (2019, 3) illustrate this through their argument that local songs and storytelling "tune with the natural environments and their dynamics," while extractive interventions weaken these practices. This finding is in line with the findings from similar studies based on other localities. This contention is even illustrated through the example provided earlier in this book about the vanishing references to forest spirits and elves in Finnish folklore, especially during the rampant development of industrialized forestry in the twentieth century. Adding a deeper ontological layer to the study of stories, Blaser (2010) provides extensive analysis on the role of storytelling based on the Yshiro and other Indigenous stories about more-than-human actors in the Paraguayan Chaco, where these actors have challenged the thinking of Western modernity. Modernity denies these realities by trying to expand developmental projects that are at odds with the Yshiro life projects. Stories of more-than-human actors are tied to particular landscapes and lived environments and have multiple meanings and functions, including for identity-building that affect the ways in which extractivism may or may not be resisted. When enclosed by extractive projects, local communities lose not only their land but also their identity, and importantly, "the local sense of belonging to the land" (Eufemia et al. 2019, 4). Yet, this is not only a story of mere meanings, or of humans de la Cadena and Blaser (2018, 2) insist, in reference to the "forest animals in Paraguay that are also spirit masters of their world," whose "destruction, perhaps unlike the destruction of nature, is hard for analysts to grasp." This resonates with the omnipresent Amerindian discourses where it is said (to global audiences) that, e.g., when a tree is cut, the spirit in it also dies (Chanchosa 2021). This provides a possible answer to the riddle presented in the Introduction about whether the more-than-human beings intimately linked with trees can survive if the trees are cut. Thus, extractivist socio-economic-cultural transformations lead to many kinds of extinctions. These extinctions need to be understood in their non-anthropocentric and inclusive diversity. It is essential to consider both the tangible and intangible extractivist world-makings and -takings, and their antidotes.

The place-identity-belonging transformations caused by extractivisms are one form of redistribution of existences, and one way to approach a slice of what is happening. There are other kinds of senses and identities, of extractivist quality, that also occur in those places. In fact, what happens at the level of local identities, habitus, customs, life-projects, and goals (especially those that young people aspire to) has a tremendous impact on the possibilities of protecting spaces from extraction, e.g., the Amazonian forests (Kröger 2020d). To explain these life-project changes, which partly enable extractivist expansion, it is useful to analyze the moral economic transformations that occur when extractivist pressure on communities is increased. Moral economic transformations can explain a great deal of how and why the extractivist pressure does not gain similar local access and support across otherwise similar contexts. The weight of the local moral economy, as conceptualized by Thompson (1963, 1971), can explain why some communities resist, and others are split when extractivist pressure increases. Of special importance is "the burden of centuries of accumulated moral economic thinking and feeling about what kinds of economic relations one should make a living by, and with whom" (Kröger 2020d, 477). Politicizing actions, framings, and personal participation in physical protests are essential for building contentious agency to counter extractivist advances, as these are transformations at both the bodily and socio-territorial-symbolic levels (Kröger 2013a). However, to be able to understand and note the different qualities of resistance, it is essential to include a deeper political ontological perspective, as resistance to extractivism is in many cases about much more than what it appears to be (as, e.g., de la Cadena (2015) emphasizes). There is a need for a greater discussion of these points, and their relation to existences, through a look at the ongoing resistance and splitting of Indigenous and other traditional communities at Amazonian and other extractivist frontiers.

Agrarian extractivisms, particularly monoculture plantations of soybeans, oil palm, and sugarcane, have recently received more focus (Alonso-Fradejas 2020; McKay 2020; McKay, Alonso-Fradejas, and Ezquerro-Cañete 2021). There is also a large literature on the soybean and other monocultures in South America, which does not explicitly utilize the concept of agroextractivism, yet it contains important theoretical underpinnings that can be used for further conceptualizing extractivisms. For example, partially similar to what I call in this book "the existentially redistributive quality of agroextractivism," Oliveira and Hecht (2016) refer to the South American soy complex as a new kind of "neo-nature." By this, they refer to "an assemblage of an exotic leguminous oilseed, selected to be amenable to mechanized planting and harvesting, adapted to longer photoperiods and higher temperatures, and able to grow in more acidic, low-phosphorus soil conditions than the temperate areas of China, the USA and Ukraine" (Oliveira and Hecht 2016, 253). They emphasize the "complete destruction of pre-existing natures" (Oliveira and Hecht 2016, 255) by neo-natures, yet retain the word "nature" in their concept to highlight that there are particular and novel, socio-environmental relations and agrarian production patterns that are expanded. In this vein, it is important to note what exactly is expanded with agroextractivisms—on top of what already existed—as a new form of life, and then consider how the specific properties of the modified life form influence existences. This analysis needs to go beyond a political economic or ecological analysis of social relations and production and consider the wider arrangement of existences. A way to access this wider arrange is through the four key questions, which are opened up in the next chapter.

Agrarian extractivisms come in many forms, each having their own particular dynamics. Forestry extractivisms based on eucalyptus, pinewood, or other tree plantations for paper pulp, energy, and other "bioeconomy" projects (Kröger 2013b, 2014, 2016b) have caused many grievances and conflicts (Kröger 2013c; Ehrnström-Fuentes and Kröger 2017). These projects have been studied as a distinct form of agroextractivism that carries its own political economy and politics (Ehrnström-Fuentes and Kröger 2018). The expansion of monoculture tree plantations, especially in Uruguay (Kröger and Ehrnström-Fuentes 2021), and the vast violations of Mapuche rights and territories in the South of Chile, have been studied through the concept of forestry extractivism (e.g., Ehrnström-Fuentes 2019). However, there is much work that can still be done to expand the scope and coverage of studying the extractivisms that are linked to tree planting and plantations. As a promising example of a new wave of forestry extractivism scholarship, González-Hidalgo, López-Dietz, and Pacheco-Pailahual (2019) show how emotional violence and remedies to the inflicted pain are essential for expanding forestry extractivism onto Mapuche lands, thus uniting political ecological analysis with an assessment of emotional dynamics. Such notions are important aspects when considering the quality of life, and how that is affected by extractivist advances.

The key issue with agroextractivisms is that they are typically monocultural. The vast monoculture plantations are extremely devastating processes when considering the scale of deforestation and the habitat losses they cause, both in both South and Central America (Kröger and Nygren 2020). Alonso-Fradejas (2020, 515) calls the sugarcane and palm monocultures in Central America "a predatory, life-purging model of agrarian extractivism." This idea of extractivism as a life-purging activity should be further studied by discussing what kind of existences, in the wide understanding of the spectrum of life, are being purged, and how. Activities, habits, and their emotional dimensions need to be studied much more carefully, and in connection with the nexus of destruction and preservation of life. Rozzi (2018), in an innovative edited book on how homogenization is operating from the viewpoint of biocultural conservation studies, emphasizes the role of destructive habits, e.g., focusing on monospecific plantations. Such monospecific habits expand homogenous monocultures, the imposition of such monocultural "habitats" over what was in a place before implying an ecocide for most, if not all, co-inhabitants of the place (the beings remaining in the agroextractivist area).

These devastating impacts of agroextractivisms have gotten worse since the spread of COVID-19, e.g., in Brazil lockdowns and other restrictions have forbidden state environmental protection agents from visiting those sites where criminal extraction has expanded. This has resulted in a not-governed setting of illegal and rampant expansion of deforesting extraction. Artacker, Campanini, and Gudynas (2020) analyze how not only Jair Bolsonaro's Brazil, but even the progressive governments, such as Luis Alberto Arce's (2020–) government in Bolivia, have continued to deepen their agroextractivist policies during the COVID-19 pandemic, lowering social and environmental regulations, and nominating deforestation-favoring politicians as ministers of environment. Thus, they try to rely on plantation, ranching, and forestry expansions as sources of what they see as development. Agroextractivisms are seen as the solution in the dire need for funds during COVID-19, especially as the dramatic fall in oil prices has led to a need to gain foreign currency quickly (Artacker, Campanini, and Gudynas 2020). These authors also emphasize that the politics during COVID-19 in South America have led to greater authoritarianism and curbing of citizen rights, which have made it harder to resist extractivist projects, and easier for the extractivists and governments to repress protestors. Prior advances and demands for more sustainable agricultural production have been sidelined, and the pandemic is seemingly producing novel and deeper rifts and divisions among red and green thinkers and politicians. To make sense of this mess, Gudynas (2020b) provides an analysis that examines which of the proposed alternatives to extractivisms are true alternatives and which not. There are several already-existing solutions in South America to the nexus of climatic, socio-ecological and health crises, such as Indigenous territories (see, e.g., de la Cadena and Blaser 2018) and the expansion of Landless Workers Movement (MST) settlements in Brazil (see, e.g., Carter 2015; Tarlau 2019; Wolford 2010), these actions are an embodiment of those practices and lived environments that are antidotes to extractivisms.

Finally, several studies treat extractivism as a global process, e.g., Dunlap and Jakobsen (2020, 6) identify "total extractivism" as "the imperative driving the global capitalist economy." They provide a nuanced and multifaceted analysis, opening up especially the role of violence caused by "the deployment of violent technologies." Ye et al. (2020) also emphasize the global character of extractivism, locating it at the core of contemporary global capitalism. However, other takes, most notably the view of Gudynas (2021), emphasizes that extractivisms always need to be place-based, and that the concept should not be conflated with an analysis of global capitalist structures or systems. Rather the concept of extractivism always needs to be used in relation to identifying particular places that are threatened, and thus, where there is potential for territorial, place-based resistance and alternatives to extractivism (Gudynas 2020a). There are many kinds of approaches to how extractivism has been and should be studied, while the above review focuses on the most recent slice of the literature from the perspective of how existences and extinctions are or are not discussed.

Extractivism is intimately tied to changes in existences, and also causes extinctions. In most cases of extractivism, everything is not totally destroyed, even if the annihilations are vast and extreme. Typically, extractivists tend to implant their own life-form of choice for the express purpose of fast and deadly capital-accumulation. By this, I mean planting cloned plant breeds, or the introduction of factory animals. With the project of capital accumulation comes monotonous work, slaughterhouses, and plantation fields, which often herald the introduction of unwanted species. These include the pests that tend to thrive in monocultures (Oliveira and Hecht 2016), and new viruses and diseases stemming from meat factories (Weis 2013). In these cases of redistributions of existences, it could be said that extractivism turns what Taylor (2015) calls "lived environments" into what Dunlap (2020, 2) calls "environments of lived erasure." In sum, the key level of focus for the study of existences and extinctions are the relations, assemblages, ensembles, meshworks (Ingold 2008), spectrums of life, and entanglements (however you wish to call them) which exist now, and how and to what extent they are being destroyed or reconfigured. As Gan et al. (2017, 4) argue:

> The problem is not just the loss of individual species but of assemblages, some of which we may not even know about, some of which

> will not recover. Mass extinction could ensue from cascading effects .... The extinction of a critical number of species would mean the destruction of long-evolving coordinations and interdependencies. While we gain plastic gyres and parking lots, we lose rainforests and coral reefs.

Actually, even more is lost, as the key explanation for continued extractivism and non-recognition of existences is to be found in metapolitics, and in the ontological shifts of not recognizing life. As the Indigenous Potawatomi plant scientist Robin Wall Kimmerer (2017: 132–133) eloquently elucidates, reflecting on the problematic ontologies taught in Biology 101 courses at universities, and on the problem of utilizing English to describe life:

> In Potawatomi 101, rocks are animate, as are mountains and water and fire and places. Beings that are imbued with spirit, our sacred medicines, our songs, drums, and even stories, are all animate ....
>
> English does not give us many tools for incorporating respect for animacy. In English, you are either a human or a thing. Our grammar boxes us in by the choice of reducing a nonhuman being to an *it*, or it must be gendered, inappropriately, as a *he* or a *she*. Where are our words for the simple existence of another living being? ...
>
> ... When we tell them [toddlers] that the tree is not a *who*, but an *it*, we make that maple an object, we put a barrier between us, absolving ourselves of moral responsibility and opening the door to exploitation. Saying *it* makes a living land into "natural resources." If a maple is an *it*, we can take up the chain saw. If a maple is a *her*, we think twice.

Indigenous people have foreseen and experienced—already quite long ago—the devastation that is now upon all of us. This devastation is due to the many runaway ecological and climate disruptions. The kind of ontological misunderstandings as noted above, which fuel this devastation, are even rooted in modern education. One example is the prophecy in the Koyaanisqatsi film, the title concept coming from the Hopis, and meaning life out of balance, a moral corruption and life in turmoil, which calls for another kind of living (Reggio 1982). Another, similar prophecy, is the already-mentioned *xawara* related by Davi Kopenawa in his book *Falling Sky*. This *xawara* can be understood as different epidemics, as physical sicknesses, or then more broadly as epidemies of evil forces, both of which were generalized with the colonialism imposed by the "white men." Epidemic *xawara*-beings were said to look like white men—which made sense, as the missionaries and conquistadors brought with them diseases and violence. Later, this negative impact has been extended to describe the general impact of modernity on the Yanomani societies and other beings, as related by Kopenawa and Albert (2013, 406):

> When the white people tear dangerous minerals out of the depths of the earth, our breath becomes too short and we die very quickly. We do not simply get sick like long ago when we were alone in the forest. This time, all our flesh and even our ghosts are soiled by the *xawara* epidemic smoke that burns us. This is why our dead shaman elders are angry and want to protect us. If the breath of life of all of our people dies out, the forest will become empty and silent. Our ghosts will then go to join all those who live on the sky's back, already in very large numbers. The sky, which is as sick from the white people's fumes as we are, will start moaning and begin to break apart.

I will continue to explore these destructive changes of existences in the next chapter by providing examples from particular extractivist activities, especially those of agrarian monocultures.

## Note

1. https://tradingeconomics.com/commodity/beef

# 2 The political economy of existences and extractivisms

Based on my personal experiences and ethnographic research, as discussed in the Introduction, and the current state of the art in extractivisms and existences scholarship reviewed in Chapter 1, I now present a more elaborated characterization of what type of natural resource extraction constitutes extractivism and to what degree. These characteristics can be understood as the key dimensions, which should be observed for each case, to identify and judge whether the activity therein should be called hyperextractivist, partially extractivist, non extractivist, or anti-extractivist. By non extractivist, I mean that instead of extracting life the activity is sustainable, equitable, and reciprocal practice based on care and respect, which augments the sphere and spectrum of what exists. An example of a non extractivist way of producing livelihoods, food, medicines, and other items needed by humans and communities are the Amazon Indigenous *chagra* home gardens and agroforestry practices (González and Kröger 2020). Anti-extractivist activities seek to actively contest extractivisms and expand the types of practices that are antidotes to extractivisms, such as those given above as examples. Another example of this kind of activity is the active expansion thrust by the Brazilian Landless Movement (MST) in many parts of Brazil of agroecological and agroforestry land reform settlements, on top of areas that were previously occupied by large landholders or targeted by extractivists, e.g., those actors seeking to expand eucalyptus plantations. There are also various degrees to extractivisms of different types. Thus, not all environmental activities of humans are extractivist in character, or extractivist in the same way, which is why I think that the concept of extractivism should not be over-extended, so that it would not lose its analytical applicability, by becoming too blurry and broad, as Gudynas (2021) has emphasized.

All, or at least most, of the below categories should be fulfilled for an activity to be labeled extractivist. This is not a binary definition,

DOI: 10.4324/9781003102977-3

as there are different degrees of extractivisms; however, when all of the categories below are clearly fulfilled (from a to d), the activity in question could be classified as hyperextractivist. When only some are fulfilled, it could be characterized as partially extractivist. I anticipate there will be differences between different economic sectors in the answer sets, as well as differences between sub-sectors and their extraction style and pace, which depends on the technologies used, extraction models, ideas, local contexts, investment politics, and global value webs. The below characterizations are processual, directing attention toward the process of expanding extractivist projects. Not all extractivist activities need to fulfill all of the categories.

Extractivisms are characterized by practices that:

a Erase most or all of the preceding life-forms, or significantly reduce their number or spectrum in the extracted area.
b Expand monocultural or monotonous life-forms over the erased places, in a redistribution of existences that significantly changes and delimits who, what, how, and for what duration in which time life-forms can exist in that area.
c Producing barren, toxic, or wasted environments, which lock-in extreme power inequalities, by making it impossible or very difficult for prior or other-than particular extractive operations to make use of the space, even if the extractive activities are discontinued.
d Create steep inequalities, whereby an elite or a political-economic sector or group, which is dominant in a bounded setting, skews the possibilities to accumulate wealth for itself, leaving for others only a limited share of the yields.

I will analyze how these four characteristics of extractivist activities are visible in different spheres of extractivisms. In addition, I offer examples of where they are not present, or only partially present. It is useful to distinguish different degrees of extractivism. I propose the following degrees, on a seven-value scale, to value how extractivist a particular set of activities are:

5 = hyperextractivist
4 = very extractivist
3 = notably extractivist
2 = partially extractivist
1 = limitedly extractivist
0 = non extractivist
–1 = anti-extractivist

Table 2.1 lists some examples of activities and the valuation of their respective levels of extractivism. It is useful to distinguish discreet activities rather than doing a regional analysis, as the same region can have varied activities that have distinct and even contrary effects. The valuations in Table 2.1 are based on my multi-sited field research. It is essential to note that the values given are not absolute, but relative, as all valuations depend on the unit of comparison and what it is being compared against. The values might change in a different comparative set. The values refer to the points of extraction/activity. In the table, n/a stands for not applicable, which in this context and set of cases is used for instances of open-pit mining, as those areas do not experience a monocultural expansion, but instead become devoid of possibilities for life altogether for a very long time. The last column refers to the overall quality that could be assigned to the activity, the evaluation considering that if extreme scores (–1 or 5) are given to two or more categories that defines the activity quality. Otherwise, average scores can be used to assess the extractivist degree of a given activity. I have only included one degree of anti-extractivism on the list, but there could also be a listing of different degrees of the anti-extractivist practice in questions, from

*Table 2.1* A comparison of different cases and a valuation of their respective levels of extractivism

| | *Characteristics of extractivism* | | | | |
|---|---|---|---|---|---|
| **Cases** | *a* | *b* | *C* | *D* | *Quality* |
| Amazon and Cerrado soy plantations | 5 | 5 | 4 | 3 | Hyperextractivist |
| Amazon illegal gold mining | 5 | n/a | 5 | 2 | Hyperextractivist |
| Eucalyptus plantations Brazil | 5 | 5 | 4 | 4 | Hyperextractivist |
| Iron ore open pits Brazil | 5 | n/a | 5 | 5 | Hyperextractivist |
| Clear-cutting forestry Finland | 3 | 4 | 1 | 1 | Partially extractivist |
| Amazon Indigenous *chagra* agroforestry | 0 | 0 | 0 | 0 | Non extractivist |
| MST settlements Brazil | 1 | 1 | –1 | –1 | Anti-extractivist |

−1 to −5, to analyze what kind of practices not only avoid contributing to or are not extractivists (0), but actively work against and try to decrease the spaces given or currently occupied by extractivisms.

Table 2.1 suggests that it is useful to separate open-pit mining and similar activities, which erase all life from a place, without introducing new life forms, as a distinct type of extractivism, with its own subcategories. So-called bioeconomies (e.g., forestry and agrarian extractivisms), and their antidotes, such as agroecological agroforestry (see Ollinaho and Kröger 2021), should be studied separately, as these are both based on introducing new life-forms to the targeted area, or expanding the scale and scope of what and who exists.

Table 2.1 also suggests that, depending on the extractivism in question, there are important differences in the possibilities to share yields. Amazonian irregular or illegal gold mining may give possibilities for a wide array of people from different backgrounds to try to earn money—if they are lucky. However, it should be noted that generally the working and human rights conditions are extremely poor in these settings, although there are notable variations in the mining worker-patron relations between Peru's Madre de Dios, Venezuela, and Brazil's different regions (Holland 2020). For example, Peru has experienced the emergence of small-scale gold mining entrepreneurs as a particular political-economic group (Cortés-McPherson 2019). In some places, miners are freer, while in others they are more bound by mafias, paramilitaries, or national political-economic elites. The values given to eucalyptus and soybean plantations seem to be equal, there are no notable differences as both are highly profit concentrating activities. However, pulp investments and their eucalyptus plantations are even more skewed and concentrated for a few corporations' mega landholdings (with some existing "outgrower" schemes) than is the case with soybean plantations (Kröger and Nylund 2012), where even relatively smaller-scale medium farmers are included to a notable degree. Iron ore extractivism is the most profit-concentrating activity, as the yields are strongly concentrated to companies like Brazilian-based Vale mining corporation, which is the world's largest interest in many minerals and metals, along with a few other global corporations.

An example of anti-extractivism is the MST settlements in Brazil. There can be negative impacts from the MST activities, e.g., when new cultivation areas are introduced, or in some rare cases when some settlements decide to plant soybean or eucalyptus (see Kröger 2013a), but the overall impact is positive. These positive impacts include the improvement of soils and current and future possibilities of life to thrive in the areas occupied by these settlements. These settlements distribute land access and control to landless peasants, as well as challenge more deeply extractivist mind-sets via particular educational curriculums, which offers an equalization of power relations (Kröger 2011; Tarlau 2019).[1]

The current clear-cutting forestry activities in Finland can be seen as partially extractivist. They are very extractivist in terms of destroying the prior forest and replacing that with a single-species tree plantation (Kröger 2016b). However, the Finnish forest ownership system is highly distributed to family forest owners (Kröger and Raitio 2017), and the use of toxic substances is stringently restricted (Kröger 2013b), which means that there are possibilities to change the land use, and thus the array of life-forms that can exist in the area. Yet, such changes would take several decades to be realized and require interventions to diversify the most monocultural tree plantation areas, which have damaged forests' multifunctionality, resilience, and recovery potential (Pohjanmies et al. 2021). However, by comparison, in Brazil's soybean and eucalyptus plantations, such sustainability transformations would be much harder, due to erosion, water depletion, use of toxic substances, and other means of land (mis)management, which renders the lands barren and makes them difficult to rewild or turn to sustainable uses (Kröger 2014; Rekow 2019). Thus, there are variations in the possibilities to revert plantation monoculture areas into sustainable uses, which depend on the baseline situation. For example, in Bahia, some eucalyptus plantation areas, which have not been used for a long time, have been successfully transformed into MST settlements and agroecological production (based on the author's field research in the area in 2004, 2006, 2008, 2011, and 2018).

An example of a non extractivist practice is the Colombian Amazonian Indigenous peoples' *chagra* agroforestry practices of cultivation, where they cultivate food, medicinal plants, and other plants for humans and other-than-humans (González and Kröger 2020), without trying to systematically expand these practices beyond their home regions in the same manner as the MST. In comparison, the MST works to expand its model in many parts of Brazil, and is also linked with Via Campesina's transnational peasant struggles against extractivisms. It also actively confronts extractivist corporations and transforms pasture and other nonproductive areas into agroecological settlements and camps. The *chagra* practice has not yet been adopted as a model by FAO or other entities (González and Kröger 2020), so it does not contribute to overall policy recommendations and has not been diffused at a larger scale. For these reasons, it is not currently an anti-extractivist model that is emulated in other contexts; however, this may change in the future. The category of non extractivism is important to highlight as there is much more than just extractivist and anti-extractivist practices. Another example of non extractivist practices are the many Indigenous regenerative livelihood and world-making practices, which exist beyond extractivist paradigms, but do not necessarily actively contest extractivist practices. Some of these practices are similar in character to the *chagra* agroforestry practices. The category of non extractivisms carries a significant amount of untapped potential for turning these practices into transformative alternatives to extractivisms, via mobilization and other political means that seek to generate transferable lessons and policies and expansion of these practices.

In each of the above cases, extractivisms, or non extractivisms, reconstitute and rearrange what exists and what can exist. It is essential to compare and explore what existed before. For example, deforestation has major consequences in terms of redistributing (and/or terminating) existences.

## Monocultures and deforestation

Agroextractivist expansions are often based on massive deforestation, like the soybean plantations in Brazil, which rely on large monocultures that are planted on top of places that once were forest. Brazil's two major frontiers of deforestation are the Cerrado and Amazon forests, which are systematically being converted into soybean plantations (Oliveira and Hecht 2016) and cattle pastures (Bowman et al. 2012; Walker et al. 2009), respectively, with the soybean expansion in the Cerrado causing the expansion of cattle ranching deeper into the Amazon (Domingues and Bermann 2012). Many ranches are later transformed into soybean plantations, with a gap of a few years between the pasture and soybean phase. The same goes for rice cultivation, which takes place either in the early years, or if soybeans are hit by a moratorium. The planters prefer rice in these instances as it helps to hide the direct link of soybean with deforestation. Yet, this system is dissolving, as new buyers, such as China's COSCO, have entered the game, and there are ways to avert the soy moratorium, which in theory demands that soy should not come from deforested areas. In November 2019, while doing field research along the BR163 highway in Southern Pará, I saw soybean fields that had been erected on the same rainforest patches that had been cleared and burned earlier that year. I saw many silos on the roadsides as well, especially COSCO's new soybean silos, which were erected very deep into the Amazon. This indicates that there are also direct deforesting processes that are initiated strictly for soybean expansion.

Deforestation rates are a proxy for the scale of eradicating lives, and the rights and possibilities of existence. There are many ways to measure shifting existences, e.g., by linking deforestation statistics with on the ground changes in existences (of different beings/or number of species) in the same place. These measures can also be taken ethnographically, by documenting how locals experience changes in what exists and does not exist anymore in a given place after an extractivist expansion. Such an account, if done through Political Ontology, could also include notes on existences that are non-modern, such as a mountain/earth-being that has been angered/churned by open-pit mining expansion (see de la Cadena 2015). This type of analysis could be accompanied by more typical research on what known life-forms exist and in what numbers they are being killed, or are rendered unable to reproduce anymore in the place of extraction. What constitutes "beings" remains at the discretion of each analyst; as Moore (2015) notes, what has been considered to be part of "nature" or "human society" has changed dramatically throughout the centuries.

The exploration of these themes is important especially now, as the territorial changes caused by (agro-)extractivisms are enormous (see, e.g., McKay 2017; Oliveira and Hecht 2016; Petras and Veltmeyer 2014; Sauer and Leite 2012). Extractivism corresponds with an equally enormous redistribution in terms who and what can exist in different places. For example, between 1988 and 2019, the total area planted with soybeans in Brazil expanded from 10.6 million hectares (Mha) to 35.9 Mha, with sugarcane increasing from 4.2 Mha to 10.1 Mha and corn from 13.4 Mha to 17.8 Mha.[2] All such expansions are reshaping several existences since they do not take place uniformly, but in certain areas targeted by particular forms of agro extractivist capital.[3] Figure 2.1 summarizes these monoculture plantation expansions.

An analysis of Figure 2.1 shows how soybean plantations expanded dramatically between 2001 and 2005. In 2006, the soy moratorium was established, after environmental organizations such as Greenpeace denounced the massive deforestation of the Amazon caused by the expansion. After this, we see that the area of soybean plantations dropped notably until 2007. However, during the same period, we see a marked increase in corn plantations, as farmers just switched to planting corn and rice for a few years, to avoid criticism. After this, they returned to planting soybean, and we see a drop in the period from 2008 to 2011 in the corn plantation area. Since 2012, there has been a huge increase in soybean cultivation, which especially targets the Cerrado. In addition, in 2004 and 2011, Lula's period in power,

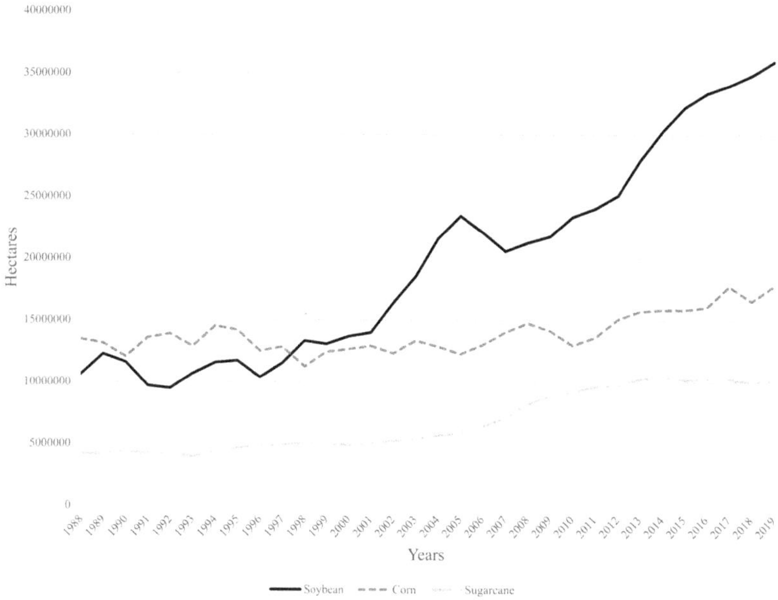


*Figure 2.1* Millions of hectares planted of soybean, corn, and sugarcane in Brazil between 1988 and 2019.
Source: Author's elaboration based on data from https://sidra.ibge.gov.br/Tabela/1612

was marked by his ethanol diplomacy, where he strongly supported the expansion of sugarcane plantations for making ethanol (although not in the Amazon, but mostly in Cerrado and Atlantic rainforest areas).

The below excerpts illustrate how land use change from forest cover to monoculture oil palm translates into on the ground changes in existences and "webs of life," which opens up in concrete terms, what existences are shifting in oil palm and tree plantation extractivisms for human and other-than-human beings. Although the below citation replicates a species-based understanding, this understanding also considers the wider web of life impacted by a species, and mentions existences and killings explicitly. These are steps to the correct direction in the path toward an "existential turn" in political economy, which is advocated for herein.

> [Many animals] are injured, killed and displaced during deforestation ... The palm oil industry has been linked to major human rights violations, including child labour ... With plantations systematically destroying the rainforest land that the local people

> depend on, communities are continuously finding themselves with no choice but to become plantation workers.[4]

The current global extractivisms, such as those done via oil palm and other monoculture expansions, lead to the annihilation of entire habitats, in an irreversible process. David Attenborough, in his Netflix documentary, *A Life on Our Planet*, describes the replacement of the Borneo rainforests with oil palm monocultures as the expansion of spaces of death over spaces where the world's richest array of life forms lives. The key point in the documentary is that one cannot consider life forms, such as humans, as separate from other beings, as they are tied together through the interconnected relations sustaining the different beings. Maintaining multitude life-forms is essential for sustaining all life on Earth, as removing species and populations at the current rate is destroying a delicate balance. Attenborough has seen these changes first-hand since the 1950s, through his career as a documentary filmmaker with a focus on nature and observing wildlife and its destructions. He explains how the five previous mass extinctions led to the vanishing of most life forms, and the same seems to be happening again, just much faster, unless actions are taken now to revert this process. This is the process of expanding extractivist practices, these being actions that cause extinctions and other serious damages. Spaces that are transformed into open-pit mines retain almost none of the original life forms in the areas impacted, and agroextractivist expansions eradicate almost all that existed before, and implant completely new, alien modified life forms. Moreover, the life that is created stems from an extractivist logic, and exists solely for the purpose of extractivist accumulation. Both the complete annihilations, and the redistributions of existences, impact the whole web of life, as the existence of all beings is based on relations with other existences and beings, not on separateness.

The thousands of square kilometers destroyed via deforestation allow some insight into the rate at which the annihilation of existences has been taking place, and are a good proxy for estimating the degree of extractivism. These places and beings have histories, which need to be opened up via detailed ethnographies, and scoping of the kcy processes and investment projects that are at the root of the most impactful and destructive cascading effects—locally, regionally, and globally. Large dam projects are one such key process (Athayde et al. 2019). In the Amazon, dam projects open up huge regions for deforestation and "industrialization," which in this case refers not to development of industries that produce added-value products, but to an expansion of ranches, sawmills, meat freezers, and monoculture plantations (Zhouri 2010). As a large number of dam-builders flock to the cities, and especially as the jobs end, these people typically end up drifting to a broader area in the same region, and investing their new earnings in their own land, which is often subsequently deforested when they set up a farm or a mine. They are being driven by the larger cattle, logging, and soybean capitalists making deals with them to do the dirty work (see Kröger 2020d). These lands are often within conservation and Indigenous areas, or otherwise robbed from peasants or traditional forest-dwellers (Higgins, 2020). This also has major existential impacts for the people already living in these areas. When the enormous Belo Monte dam was constructed, the required flooding and growing pressure to deforest, caused the Brazilian public prosecutor Thais Santi to argue that Belo Monte is an Indigenous ethnocide (Brum 2014) as the people living there lose the lived environment upon which their existence is based. The speech by Munduruku Chief Jairo Saw on May 11, 2015, criticizing Amazon dam projects illustrates how there can be different understandings of what and who should have the right to exist among the various Brazilian social actors. "We are a part of the nature: we do not want that our knowledge disappears, our form of living, of organizing. We want that you respect us, that the world knows what we are feeling" (Lila 2015).[5]

There are heated debates and emotions around the world that center on extractive operations and the destruction they bring. Even in the Global North, e.g., in Finland, mining and forestry projects and extractions have brought to the surface many conflicting viewpoints on the eradication of existences. For example, one commentator notes (Elonen 2019), in relation to a news piece on birds vanishing due to clear-cutting in Finnish forests, that:

> I feel shocked by the felling of forests, because birdlife is reduced … insects and micro-organisms vanish, and then vanish also the birds. In Southern Finland there are no forests. But the destruction of forests is … related to the climate. Forests are also an issue related to human wellbeing. [6]

The commentary above reflects the rising complaint that forests are still primarily used by the forestry sector for productivist aims, especially for pulping and energy wood, although some advances have been made in diversifying forestry practices (Kröger and Raitio 2017). Many question whether the current tree base in Finland can even be conceived of as a forest, this skepticism a result of the deeply ingrained plantation-centric model of forest management (Hyvärinen 2020), wherein Finland is a world-systemic core country actively expanding the global expansion of tree plantations through financing, technology, consulting, diplomacy, and foreign investments (Kröger 2013b). Ecological studies concur, e.g., in the sense that while there is still a large tree base, species are vanishing from the forests (Kotiaho 2017). Ilkka Hanski (2000), who was the leading forest ecologist in Finland, argued that the heavy deforestation in Finland has created an extinction debt, which is getting worse as continuous forest areas are becoming rarer, and more forest areas are degraded, fragmented, clear-cut, or deforested. Meanwhile, in Latin America, the situation is even more dire, as the extractivisms there are not partial, but hyperextractivist.

## Toward an existential political economy

The need to more directly link political-economic and ecological analysis with the analysis of existences is growing evermore crucial, as the pace of extractivism increases. A historical change has taken place in the last 10–20 years at both the local and global level, leading to massive new land grabbing (Edelman, Oya, and Borras 2013). This land rush is a form of resource grabbing that increases the metabolic rift, which is the amount of raw materials created for industrial uses. This process is taking place around the world, even in the Arctic, whose case exemplifies how new mining projects need to target weaker deposits, as the richest resource bases have already been depleted (Kröger 2019). This has led to a tenfold increase in the amount of side-rock (waste) excavated in comparison to the actual minerals and metals extracted at Finnish mining sites (Kröger 2016). This suggests that capitalism is having serious trouble reproducing what Moore (2015) calls "cheap natures," and therefore also in producing profits. Moore (2015) has argued that the end of cheap natures signals the end of capitalist expansion, which necessitates the creation and appropriation of cheap natures as commodities. The change in the volume of the tangible world and landscapes that resource extraction must radically transform to be able to produce the same amount of commodities as previously possible has major consequences for the beings whose homes depend on the continued existence of those places. These homes are being destroyed in greater quantities as the expropriative processes get more wasteful, and use more land less efficiently. This kind of understanding about the interface of commodity production, value, capital accumulation, and existences is needed to rethink and refocus attention to the lives, and possibilities and spaces for the future lives that could be lost through these processes.

Extractivisms, including the capitalist, "progressive," e.g., "communist" (as in the Soviet Union), or contemporary South American "socialist" (as in Venezuela) processes within the modernity of industrial-scale landscape transformation, work through a violent struggle at the physical sites of existential redistributions and destructions. This is visible in the discussion around neo-extractivist models, which grasped the attention of most early scholars of extractivism (as an economic model), and came to define the period of 2000s–2010s in Latin America, wherein even so-called progressive governments started to embrace policies of furthering commodity exports and resource extraction, rooting their other policies to serve this cornerstone of their macroeconomic and political models (Gudynas 2015; Svampa 2019).

Besides giving attention to extractivism's macro-economic and other political-economic impacts, including their political ecological dimensions, I argue that it is crucially important to place further emphasis on the extractivist activities ushered in during the 2000s commodity booms, as particular ways of producing lived environments and "nature" that is, life (and its ontologies). These changes ought to be linked to distinct projects of redistributing and reshaping existences. This does not mean that we could and should not still continue to explain the power relations behind extraction using the classic analytical elements in political economy, which according to Foweraker (1981) include the study of modes of production, the mechanisms of accumulation, and the expropriation of surpluses by particular actors, as well as surveying the wide range of political, legal, and ideological interventions by the state.

Extractivisms violently transform landscapes. Seeing such landscape alterations is helpful in directing increased attention to the following key questions: (1) who or what exists, can exist, and/or has the right to exist; (2) how they can exist (the quality of the existence); (3) in which time do they have the right to exist in this space (before and after the extractive operations); and (4) who are the key entities deciding and contesting the rights to exist? For example, soybean, sugarcane, and eucalyptus monocultures can be identified as areas wherein existences are limited to only a few species, whose life span (rotation) is quite short (in terms of modernity's conception of time), and who are tied to complex global commodity networks that produce human and animal suffering (e.g., via the feed complexes). This suffering is not created without also causing damage in the classic political-economic sense. As a political-economic consequence of extractivist expansions, Marques (2007, 2012) argues that the Amazon is being fixed as a mineral-energetic colony for the rest of the country and multinational production capital. Furthermore, Brazil's economy is becoming increasingly reliant on raw material exports, which has damaging impacts on social welfare and equity (Young 2017).

Marx (1976 [1867], 522) observed that "capital comes [into the world] dripping from head to foot, from every pore, with blood and dirt," which is a good basis for an existential political economy. In terms of existences, deforestation signifies radical decimations—what was before in one place is there no more. In addition, often what was not in one place before is there now, and in massive quantities, with short lifespans (such as monocultures). There is also a creative side to extractivisms, especially in relation bioeconomic extractivisms, which are based on agricultural or plantation commodities. It is this creation, which is seen as the only approved form of "production" and thus the best example of "productivity," that is the key to explaining the acceptability of extractivist activities. These extractivists suggest that something "productive" was able to replace the "non-productive," "empty" spaces, and thus yield something good, an improvement, a development.

These violent colonial expansions are not possible without legitimizing actions and discourses, which rely on recasting what exists and using new words and new meanings for words, such as production. This was already the case with the nineteenth-century US conquest of the West (Smith 2008). The creation of the idea of a void space—wherein there would not be any lived environments or existences—is essential when hiding the violence of the process. Another legitimizing tactic is the discourse of endless space. In Brazil, the elites deny that there could be a lack of land (May 1999), and they try to emphasize, through their publications and direct participation in the drafting of legislation, the minimal and relatively insignificant size of the land they are transforming. Martins (1984) argues that the Brazilian landed elites see the land as a void site for private wealth-creation—a view that still corresponds with the monoculture landscape of existence following in the wake of contemporary deforesters.

Enclosure also results in new modes of (human) being, e.g., by turning ex-servants into beggars and robbers (Marx 1976 [1867]). In this Marxian value perspective, production not only creates new commodities but also refashions the relations between humans and other-than-humans in their environments, meaning that changes in production are reflected in socio-environmental relations (see Turner 2008). In a similar way, the array of existences is strongly impacted by the type of processes that shape the landscape. On par with Marx's notion of the creative power of enclosure, the monocultures of agroextractivisms expand one or a few kinds of existence in an enclosed area, e.g., cattle and pasture grass, or soybean and corn. Even hydrocarbon and mining extractivisms expand some forms of life at the cost of others, such as the humans operating the mining or drilling machineries at the points of extraction. The notion of existential redistributions is helpful for assessing these existential changes, but it is even more useful when considering the cascading political-economic transformations related to existential transformations—locally and globally.

Extractivism is not only a destructive process but also a spatial process that creates or offers space for new existences—although mostly in a manner which radically decreases the scope of what can exist, and how. Even an open-pit mine, which uses heavy toxics and causes long-term toxicity and barren landscapes—thus barring the possibilities of life in most of its forms to root or be based on that area—does open up the possibility for some humans to work in the area for a few years. However, it is not the case that their existence would be based on that area, as their food and water come from outside of the area, as almost no life can be supported by those areas. Yet, these extractivist open-pit areas do promulgate the expansion of human habitation in other, nearby areas, and it is not uncommon to see some of the wealth remain via miners who leave the mining activity and use the gains to establish farming or ranching livelihoods. Existential changes should be studied in different areas, to see the impacts more broadly.

By the concept of existential redistributions, I want to direct attention to how the utilization and modification of life-forms, and lived environments are essential for one's analysis, to be able to better understand political-economic and political ecological changes. While there have been some inroads in this direction in recent scholarships, as reviewed in Chapter 1, much more can still be done to strive toward a post-Cartesian framework for scientific analyses (see Haraway 2004). Next, I will provide a concrete analysis of a regionally situated world-ecological transformation to open up what I mean by a political economy of existences.

## Agroextractivism of northern Mato Grosso, and existential redistributions

The first changes that agroextractivist expansions create in many parts of the Cerrado and the Amazon are the decimations of existing Indigenous peoples and the forests they inhabit. The 1970s "frontier" expansions into the Amazon by Brazil's dictatorship were based on full-scale extinctive and even genocidal drives. I will first offer an example of these human losses, tying these to broader explanation of what the logging-ranching-soybean extraction meant for northern Mato Grosso's existing populations. This account of how northern Mato Grosso was colonized by Southern Brazilians of European-descendant in the 1970s contextualizes and historicizes the setting that I will use as a basis for applying the four key questions in Chapter 3.

During my multi-sited political ethnography on the causalities of deforestation in the Amazon, I did field research in November and December 2019 along the BR163 Highway running from Cuiabá to Santarém in Brazil. In the northern part of the Mato Grosso State, I talked with a member of the almost-extinguished Panará Indigenous people. The Panará met the fury of the "resource frontier," which was how the Amazon was framed in the 1970s by the dictatorship. The military government ordered a highway to be built through the dense rainforest areas inhabited by the Panará. At this time, they had little or no outside influences or contacts. Currently, these areas are large soybean plantations where one cannot see the end of the fields, just empty horizons. The central village of the Panará was located in what is today the center of the large city of Sinop, in Mato Grosso. The name of the city comes from the first letters of *Sociedade Imobiliária Noroeste do Paraná* (The Northeastern Paraná Real Estate Company), which was the name of the corporation from the southern Paraná state that was given the right by the dictatorship to colonize northern Mato Grosso by bringing in farmers with predominantly European origin from Paraná. Figure 2.2, from July 1973, illustrates what the baseline situation of the landscape was when this "frontier expansion" began. The landscape changes are quite stark. This expansion turned the Panará's homes into white men's "real estate," as Figure 2.2 shows the first city grid being laid into the rainforest, right on the place where the Panará Indigenous peoples' central village was located.

To see Sinop today, one would hardly know that there had once been an extensive forest in the same space the city now occupies. The landscape changes that have taken place in less than 50 years are shocking. There are now highways, broad avenues, and concrete buildings with only tiny slices of urban forest.[7]

To have an idea of what the areas close to this region look like now, after extractivisms have dramatically transformed the landscapes, Figure 2.3 was taken by me in a soybean field about 20 km south of Sinop along the BR163, on November 19, 2019.

*Figure 2.2* The grid for the city is carved into the Amazon forest.
Source: Assentamento SINOP, Julho de 1973, às margens da BR-163. Foto aérea Acervo Fotográfico TenCelJaimeRibeiro. https://commons.wikimedia.org/wiki/File:1973Jul,BR163, ColonizacaoSINOP.jpg CC BY-SA 4.0.

*Figure 2.3* A ground level view from a soybean field. Soybeans almost as far as the eye can see.
Source: Photo taken by the author.

I visited a middle-aged survivor of the Panará tribe, Nikré Panará Guarantã, to interview him in Portuguese (which should be noted was not his mother tongue, I have made the translation into English) about the experience of the 1973 transformation on their lives:

> When the highway was built no one knew what roads or tractors were. So, they opened up highways running from Cuiabá to Santarém and this brought many problems to the Panará people. When the highway came, people started to die, I do not know if they [the colonizers] spread something, maybe poison, and many people died! Died suddenly, and this illness did not take even a day [before one] died, it took [only] one, two hours to die, so this brought many problems for the community and very few survived .... Only 70, 75 people survived ... especially from flu.

This was a catastrophic decline in Panará peoples' lives to just 70–75 persons. This decimation of the Panará population illustrates how extractivist megaproject proponents, such as the colonizers of Mato Grosso, decide who can live and where. The surviving 75 people were moved elsewhere, to an area already inhabited by another Indigenous group, and their descendants were returned to an area closer to their original territory only in the 1990s. No other Indigenous tribe speaks or understands their language. This was an ethnocide and ecocide of major proportions, removing the lived environments, their existences, and the place-based understandings of those who existed. Nikré also reflected on these broader changes that building the highway and colonization meant for the Panará. These are illustrative of the extinctions of existences.

> This region had tall forest, a place where bows were of use, and today this is not here, so we perceive that today grass substitutes forest and this leaves a person very sad. I see [our] people planting for the large farmer, it was not like this because the forest itself was tall, one knew where the place to cultivate was, knew that where there is high forest, [that area] is for hunting and there are many fruits. Today we do not see anything anymore, and this is left very clear by the people, especially by the old who walked here and know this region. They know of the place, even without the forest, even with the grass that has substituted the forest, they remember of this place, know where there is game, where to hunt turtle. Today it is difficult, the population increased, and we have to hunt very far and fish also [very far], because the river today is

> drying each time more because of deforestation. For this reason, we do not manage to hunt or fish anymore, and especially in the dry season it is very difficult, very dry, and in this one does not manage to walk. In the past year a problem occurred, many fish died, we do not know why so many fish died! This deforestation leaves the community very preoccupied.

This state of Mato Grosso uses seven times more pesticides than the average in Brazil (Rede Cerrado n.d.), due to being the world capital of soybean production. Large amounts of pesticides are used in an ever-increasing diversity in Brazil's fields, and the Bolsonaro government approved over 1,000 new pesticides during its first two years (Pedlowski 2021). This is dire development not only for those who are sickened or die due to pesticide exposure, but it is also harmful for the country's trade balance and development (Giovanaz 2020). These monocultures can be seen principally as fields of death. The killing of all other beings and living organisms, except the growing soybean, corn, or cotton (the latter two are used as cover crops when the soybean is not grown) is the basis of the continued existence of the commoditizing process. Nearby, surviving human populations are also affected by this poisoning. For example, in the town of Lucas do Rio Verde, next to Nova Mutum, glyphosate has been found in 100 percent of the mother's milk in the region according to scientific studies (Weissheimer 2016). The World Health Organization's (2016) research has classified glyphosate as "probably carcinogenic to humans," and other researchers in South America have assessed the many negative impacts this high use of pesticides has in the region (e.g., Oliveira and Hecht 2016). The high use of pesticides has locked-in a very deadly global agribusiness model (Clapp 2021). To keep the machine of agribusiness running, it is very hard to take away a piece, like the use of pesticides, even with the knowledge that the tradeoff to grow this crop is killing everything else in the area and poisoning the region.

Northern Mato Grosso has been transformed in a matter of few decades from a place that was sustainably inhabited by the Panará Indigenous people, and all others living in these Amazon-Cerrado transition forests, into killing fields of vast monoculture plantations. The aforementioned example is primarily and most importantly a case that illustrates this redistribution. However, most studies of this region have not taken this approach, but focused instead on so-called agricultural modernization, the success of Brazil's soybean expansion into the North, and other economistic or Western modernist accounts. The next chapter illustrates how a political economy of existences, through the four key questions, can offer a more balanced, inclusive, and just explanation of what has happened, and is happening in this region.

## Notes

1. However, whether these MST efforts succeed depends greatly on the contextually-specific moral economies, there are great divergences between Southern and Northeastern Brazil in this regard (Wolford 2010). Thus, the study of anti-extractivisms need to be firmly grounded in moral economic analysis based on contextual understandings of what constitutes anti-extractivist actions and how these could be attained across varying historical settings and extractivist impetuses.
2. Data from https://sidra.ibge.gov.br/Tabela/1612 (accessed March 13, 2021).
3. Histórias do Cerrado, a new online portal, accessibly documents the devastations caused by these and other deforesting expansions in different parts of Brazil's Cerrado. https://redecerrado.org.br/historiasdocerrado/en/mato-grosso/
4. https://www.livepuresoap.com/why-palm-oil-free/ (accessed March 13, 2021).
5. Author's translation from Portuguese.
6. Author's translation from Finnish.
7. The physical changes in the space Sinop occupies between the 1970s and today are extensive. See https://alchetron.com/Sinop,-Mato-Grosso for an aerial view of the city.

# 3 Four key questions for the study of existences

## The agroextractivist monocultures in Mato Grosso

Based on my empirical observations and the existing research I have reviewed in this book; I propose four key questions for studying existences:

1 Who or what exists?
2 How they can exist (what is the quality of existence)?
3 In which time and/or how long can they exist?
4 Who are the key entities deciding and contesting the rights to exist?

I will next assess each of the four key questions in detail and offer examples for each of them. When conducting a political economy of existences, from the viewpoint of how extractivist expansions and projects influence existences, it is useful to focus on processes. I will continue from the aforementioned context of northern Mato Grosso; whose dynamics of change constitute a major existential transformation. By this, I mean the decimation of the Indigenous peoples and the eradication of most forests, which was caused by the colonization from the Paraná state in the 1970s. This colonization has had drastic impacts on the array of who and what has the possibility to be born and live in that area now.

As said, when assessing the four key questions, it is important to reflect on them through a processual view. In this, the concept of frontier is helpful, as it emphasizes a process and movement in time and place, rather than a standing moment in a static place. From the frontier perspective, the four key questions can be further framed with the following details:

- How is the distribution of who and what can exist changed by the extractivist process?
- What is the quality of existence like for those who exist in the area?

DOI: 10.4324/9781003102977-4

- For how long can those who exist in the place live? How is the conception and rhythm of time transformed? For how long does the extractivist process seem to continue?
- Who are the key entities deciding and contesting the rights to exist?

These questions need to be asked for each of the meaningful, key places where existences are redistributed by an extractivist chain. I will focus on observing how the soybean agroextractivist process affects existences at the point of extraction, at the plantation sites, by comparing what existed in the place prior to extractivism to the moment of eradications of existences. I will then examine what exists there now, and how those arrangements are being transformed within the continuing extractivist process in that locality.

For a full account of a detailed global political economy of existences, one also needs to ask the same questions along the whole commodity chain or value web. In this case, this would include: the logistical pathways, such as the road, railroad, port, and maritime localities; the processing facilities located in other physical places, such as slaughterhouses and industrial facilities; the further processes, where the commodities are used or consumed, such as supermarkets and homes; and, the afterlives of what is left of the life and beings that are transformed into commodities, such as garbage piles and recycling operations. As such this analysis would be very extensive. My recommendation for single researchers is to focus on a specific sector (e.g., mining), and its particular sub-sector and commodity (e.g., gold), and even more precisely to the specific style of extraction (e.g., open-pit, illegal and irregular, mercury-using, deforesting, and violent gold mining), taking place in a particular place, context, polity, political-economic system, and regionally situated world-ecology (e.g., a particular conservation unit or region in the Amazon, or a set of these within a group of cases which can be compared due to some essential contextual qualities that the cases share, in a particular period of time or a historical process). Multi-sited ethnography and process-tracing can be used as methods to uncover these dynamics, following the methodological examples provided in Tsing (2015), Gan et al. (2017), and Kröger (2020a, 2021).

To answer the four key questions, I focus both on what was in the area before, and what is there now, analyzing the transformative processes based on the accounts of the key actors who are expanding the frontier.

## Who or what exists?

The point of extraction that I use as an example herein are the soybean/corn plantations of farm owner Marcos Ioris, located about 20–30 km to the east and southeast of the town of Nova Mutum, along the BR163 highway in northern Mato Grosso, Brazil. Marcos is considered to be a medium-sized farm owner in the area with the 20 workers on his farm, but in a broader comparison, he is an agribusiness millionaire running major operations. Ioris has been politically active in the soybean producers' associations. He cultivates two soybean fields, one owned by him, which is 1,200 hectares, and another one, which he rents from absentee owners in São Paulo, which is 5,000 hectares. According to him, there were a lot of people who bought land cheaply in the 1970s and were now just leasing these lands to be used as farms for others to open and cultivate, as they did not want to maintain the infrastructure and live in the area. I visited the field areas with him, and also the offices and soybean and corn silos of the cooperative company of which he owns a quarter.

When I first visited the soybean fields on November 18, 2019, the sun was setting, and it was very quiet. Only the sound of wind could be heard, and the visual experience in the fields was striking. One could see only a flat horizon where a few years ago there had been a dense forest, a mixture of the Cerrado and Amazon forests, as this was a transition zone between the two biomes. Figure 3.1 captures my first moments on the fields at the farm that Ioris named Palotina, after his hometown in the Paraná state.

Existential transformations are visible in Figure 3.1 and landscape, as well as in the names. In this new version of Paraná's Palotina, there is quite recently planted soybean, and a dirt access dirt, as well as the soybean field owner, observing the genetically modified (GM) soybeans. Marcos indicated that these soybean seeds came from Bayer. In the far distance, one can see the soybean handling facilities, and a small remnant of forest. As illustrated by Figure 3.1, the scene is the same in whichever direction one looked as there was practically nothing else to be seen. For Marcos himself, this scenery opened up in the following way:

> Here in fact is a soybean crop, planted in early October. The rains are generous this year, the rainy season began in early October and it is doing really well, we can even tell it rained yesterday and today, and crops are developing well. We plant this

*Figure 3.1* The producer looks over his fields of soy. A seemingly endless flat horizon that once was forest.
Source: Photo taken by the author.

> crop in October to harvest in February. Then, we remove this crop and plant corn, in the same area. You plant corn and harvest in June, so, in the same rainy season, that is from October to April, we can have two crops without irrigation. Our climate here is suitable for that, because there is a regime of 2,000 to 2,400 millimeters of rain in this period, so we managed to have these two crops. Some producers plant cotton in succession to soybeans, but these are the largest producers, producers with a scale of industries [over 100,000 hectare plantations], the standard producer in the region works with soybean and corn succession, which is a very good practice for being direct planting. There is no erosion or soil revolving, you have organic matter that improves productivity every year, then a crop like this, except for any weather problem, will produce 65 bags per hectare that are 3,600–3,900 Brazilian real [(BRL), which would be about 775–840 euros at the exchange rates on November 18, 2019], about this range, depending on the variety, depending on the time of harvest. So, I think the crop is there, our part is now done, the weather has to do its part.

The above points about these plantations improving the soil and not causing erosion are not exactly factual, and I will come back to them below. As a continuation to the above question, I asked about how much profit he can make with these harvests:

> Producing soybeans and corn we will make a profit, taking out the inputs and investments, we make around 1,200,000 BRL [258,595 euros] a year, between soybean and corn, 100,000 BRL [21,550 euros] a month, approximately depending on the price of the product, in certain years, maybe more or less than that.... That's the profit for this property, this 1,200-hectare property.

Then, I asked what was here before the soybean plantations. To my surprise, and revealingly of the type of thinking of existences, Marcos replied that:

> Before this, there was corn. We took the corn out in June and the straw stayed there, when it starts raining, we plant soybeans, so here the model is taking the soybean out, planting corn, taking the corn out, planting the soybean.

After giving the primary importance to soybeans and corn, he continued:

> Before the implementation of the crop, there was Cerrado. We explored it within the law. If you look further there, there is a forest, our legal reserve. We have 20 percent of the area as a reserve according to the legislation in force; at the time, we could explore 80 percent. We planted rice in the first year, then soybean and corn.

It is essential to note that all the crops planted here—soy, corn, and cotton—are cloned and tailored for agroextractivist processes. This process of genetic "enhancement" has drastically narrowed the variety of both crop and animal breeds (Weis 2013, 95).

As the interview continued, I returned to the issue of how the region was before, and what is there now. I explained that this was my first time to visit northern Mato Grosso, and I could not imagine how the place looked before the plantations. Marcos' reply gives an understanding of the extension of the area that is similar to the above picture, the plains with endless soybean plantations:

> This here for me, this large plateau that extends all the way from here to Sapezal and Campo Novo, is a large plateau of three million hectares that is all like this, except where there is water. If you

> know those regions [with water], they are even more beautiful in comparison to these plains.

According to the existing research, there are wild animals living in the border forests of the soybean and corn plantations in Mato Grosso who cause considerable economic losses to crop planters. Most notable is the white-collared peccary (WLP), also known as a musk hog, but in contrast to the local farmers' claims in my interviews of not trying to kill the animals, Lima et al. (2019) find that farmers currently use poisons to control the populations of peccaries and other beings that could be perceived to damage the yield. It is useful to see this poisoning through the frontier logic, as this is a process with a frontier-like, expanding and cascading, processual effect, where the applied poison continues its existentially destructive function beyond the first place of introduction, causing collateral damages, and expanding the damages far beyond the targets of killing. Lima et al. (2019, 37) describe how:

> Poisoning is usually achieved using the product "Furadan," a nematicide insecticide...Farmers first habituate WLPs to eat salt deposited in troughs in the forest. Once WLPs become preconditioned to the feeding site, farmers poison the troughs. We received several independent reports of this technique and in one case more than a hundred animals were killed at once, likely subsequently contaminating forest scavengers such as king vultures ... and two species of turkey vultures ...
>
> This indiscriminate method has grave consequences as many non-target species including tapir ... and brocket deer ... are also attracted to salt and die along with WLPs. Carnivores and carrion consumers that subsequently feed on the poisoned carcasses often succumb in turn ...

The authors also suggest that the peccaries should be saved due to their existence being very useful and supportive for a large array of other existences, and warn that "until protective measures are taken, these superb Neotropical ecosystem engineers will continue to be decimated within agribusiness landscapes, in which many farmers favour their eradication rather than their control" (Lima et al. 2019, 37).

As the night was setting in over the vast open fields, I continued to ask Marcos about the transformative process:

MARKUS KRÖGER (MK): And what type of vegetation was there here, what size of trees?

MARCOS IORIS (MI): It was Cerrado.
MK: But how was this, as I never saw it?
MI: The Cerrado has a few distorted trees of two to three meters height and grass beneath them.

At this point I became suspicious, as I had seen photographs and heard that the trees in this area had been much taller. In fact, taking into account the scope of the existing literature, from remote sensing and other sciences, there are major questions around the claim that the Nova Mutum region would even be pure Cerrado. This area is a transitional zone between the Cerrado and Amazon biomes, and includes vegetation from both, which has created challenges when studying deforestation in the area. This same transitional area is also called the "arc of deforestation," and Nova Mutum is located within it, and it "plays an important role in the context of deforestation in the frontier of Amazon and Cerrado" (de Souza Mendes et al. 2019, 1161). According to de Souza Mendes et al. (2019, 1161):

> … the Cerrado biome in Brazil covers three main vegetation types: grassland, savannas, and forest formations, which results in indeterminate boundary and a gradient of biomass, height, and tree cover. This large variance in different types of vegetation in the Cerrado is responsible for the high biodiversity in this biome.

There is a large microclimate variability and many different types of soils, in sum a "large biodiversity and floristic heterogeneity" (de Souza Mendes et al. 2019, 1161). In Nova Mutum, de Souza Mendes et al. (2019) disclose that all the naturally dominate vegetation types are some sort of forests, including Open Forests, Dense Woodlands, gallery forests, and secondary forests. The height of the trees in these types of forests vary between 5 and 30 m, so the claim of only 2-to-3-meter high trees does not appear to be true.

In general, the Cerrado biome has an astonishing variety of life forms and relations that are unique. There are over 8,500 native terrestrial species, over 7,000 of these being plants; moreover, 44 percent of the plants and 28 percent of the amphibians are endemic, which are unusually high proportions of endemism. In 2016, there were 59 plants and 55 animals found to be close to extinction, with the expectation of further extinctions rapidly expanding if plantation expansion continues (Zenni, Guimarães, and Tidon 2019).

As I was aware of the richness of what had been lost in Nova Mutum, I continued the questions after the above reply from Marcos (however, without explicitly questioning his claims) to gather an understanding of how the locals perceived the area as it was, what exists there now, and the transformations. The above notes on the accuracy of the factual claims, and other types of perceptions, are presented to avoid passing disinformation or a single viewpoint. These notes are intended to provide an array of answers to the main question of this section: Who or what exists? This question is then followed up with additional insight on how this has changed in the area and in the time under investigation.

MK: And was it possible to walk in there?

MI: Yes, it was possible to enter into the middle, it was not a closed dense forest, the forests are close to the water sources, and where there is better land, at lower altitudes.

MK: And what did you do in these Cerrados before?

MI: We came here to explore, I did not live here in the past, I came from Paraná. I arrived, acquired a property to explore, when I arrived, I soon dismantled those trees and grasses, put the limestone and started to produce, the old people who lived here had pastures used to produce cattle.

MK: When you arrived, were there already cattle here?

MI: Not on this property, but around it, yes.

This answer indicated to me that this was an area directly deforested from the Cerrado–Amazon transition forest. The next day, we visited another plantation area, and I continued to ask questions, many of them similar to the above, but slightly altered, to see if the answers varied. This would help me to understand what a soybean producer understood to exist in these areas, and how his life had been living here. Marcos explained that when he arrived in this region, "the government encouraged us to explore the land, because it was a very unproductive region." He had personally witnessed the transformations of the region almost from the beginning and had participated in them. I asked him how the process was from his viewpoint.

MK: So, you said that when you arrived, there were 5,000 people and now, there are about 50,000, how is life here, could you talk a little about this process, what you experienced?

MI: In the beginning, it was difficult, you know, there was no energy, there were no highways. In the beginning, this project was a 150,000-hectare project of a colonizer who brought the children

> of producers from the South, from Paraná, who had this aptitude for agriculture, because the people of Mato Grosso do not have this ability, you know. So, the project in this region started with livestock, which opened the Cerrado, putting the grass for livestock [in the 1970s]. But after this [in the 1980s], the gauchos, the people who came later, said we have to plant, [due to the area's] topography, it rained a lot, [the region] has good rain, and [the colonizers] began to dominate the planting of soybeans and rice. First rice, right, in the Cerrado, limestone, such, shovel, shovel, there, the research came, began to develop varieties of soybeans suitable for the tropical region, [for] that productivity started to increase, right, then came agriculture, came companies, and then the region started to develop, right.

It is important to pay attention to the first items mentioned in the above passage, as a reflection of the worldview of the soybean producers about the quality of life in a historic sense. The two first things that are mentioned as *lacking* are energy and highways. These do now exist in the area. They did not exist there before. The extractivisms taking place in the area would not exist without these infrastructures. The first question—in what I call a political economy of existences—refers not only to *who* exists and existed in an area but also *what* exists and existed.[1] Notably, the above passage also suggests that the colonizers saw (and see) their role as racially or ethnically required, with claims that the people already living in the area would not have the "ability" to "develop" the region by expanding ranching.

After I asked Marcos details about the deforestation in that area, he tried to defend his land use, arguing that of this rented farm, he had opened only 5,000 hectares, and not the rest of the 14,000 hectares, which are located at lower altitudes that are still forest and savannah, not in the high plains. He said that he opened the 5,000-hectare plantation in a single stroke, as this was easier, not piece-by-piece. In practice, he did this in the following way:

> In practice, you have two tractors with a chain between them and you go on felling down [them], because they are not trees. . .they are not trees. . .you lay [them] on the ground. Then, you take a tractor with a fork and make a "windrow," and pile it up. Then, we used fire to eliminate this what was here, right.

He also said that when he came to Nova Mutum, there used to be much more Cerrado, where "we even came to hunt pigeons, hunt birds … and, in that time, there were many, we came here to give some shots on the birds." However, he did not seem to be sad or sorry for the loss of this possibility, or the birds.

The next day, when visiting the larger 5,000 hectares farm, there was a group of company researchers collecting samples of pests and diseases in the soybean fields. We had come to take a look at a new poisoning tractor that had been purchased recently for the cost of 630,000 BLR (about 135,000 euros). This tractor ran quickly over the rows, poisoning everything in its path (Figure 3.2).

There were countless life-forms being killed that day in front of our eyes and under our noses, as the tractor spread poison over the huge field, running at 60–80 km per hour. Marcos explained how it is a constant race to try to develop what he called "defensives" against the ever-developing pests and diseases that have become resistant to pesticides (see Clapp 2021; Shattuck 2021). Monocultures tend to create the need for different kinds of pesticides, fungicides, herbicides, bactericides, and disinfectants, which can be spread on top of the plantations or inserted directly into the GM crops. The very presence of the monocultures and decreased biodiversity create conditions where pests are transformed and redefined at the species level as a threat to the crops (Weis 2013). These same species would not be pests in high biodiversity settings, as the diversity balances out the potential harmful effects of any one specific species or type of species (Altieri 2018).

*Figure 3.2* The new tractor, poisoning the fields.
Source: Photo taken by the author.

Thus, monoculturization leads to a redistribution and transformation of almost all the existences it touches or where it is based, which also includes the forms of life it uses as its agents. The role and meanings of what existed before are transformed when a place experiences a shift to the monoculturization drive. I have included some photos of the beings, which the soybean producers call pests and order to be killed (see Figures 3.3 and 3.4).

New machineries also entered the business. Marcos commented on the necessity to take big loans to buy the new machines, thus making him accrue debt. By way of example to illustrate the perceived value

*Figure 3.3* One of the beings whose existence is intolerable due to the perception of it being "dangerous invader" that threatens potential profits.
Source: Photo taken by the author.

*Figure 3.4* Another one of the beings that manages to exist in the soy fields, but will be dispatched whenever possible.
Source: Photo taken by the author.

and importance of these machines, BMWs are very rare, expensive, and exclusive cars in Brazil, and they seemed to be a topic and scale of valuation that was discussed often between the soybean farmers in the town. These poisoning machines cost the same as three BMWs. New technologies were also often arriving, including those that would make it possible to poison the fields without humans needing to physically drive the machines, even at night, and seemingly without human errors.

> … instead of overlapping or crossing [the same path the machine has already passed], it stops automatically. It does a reading, so as not to overlap, it doesn't cross … it is very practical … it will be monitored by control, you will program it, map the area, the only thing you will do is supply the planter [with seeds] or put the product [pesticide] inside.

This arrival of automatic machineries will further narrow the scope of what exists, and also cause major changes to the rhythm and variability of life and impact of humans on the environment. Fewer humans will be needed to run the agricultural system. Having fewer jobs available on the plantations, will cause the workers and their families to leave the area in search of work. Those who do stay to work will need to physically come to the plantation less often as more processes are automated. Perhaps, these workers will not even need to visit the plantations in the future at all, but will be more akin to programmers, running the machines from a far. Thus, human presence in the towns and the regions continues to diminish as jobs vanish and work relations fundamentally change through increased automation. Although he was fascinated by the new technology and waiting for it to arrive, Marcos saw that the arrival of the new technologies that did not need humans as operators would "create conflicts."

> I think it's bad, because how much labor will it take? ... I think this process has to happen, but not at a very high speed, governments have to prepare themselves, for example, more and more people will be retired, living on the government ... [so how does] a person have services, a job ...

In the middle of our discussion, as we drove in the same car away from the soybean fields and toward the town, we saw a few large birds running in the fields. Marcos explained that these were rheas, which partially co-exist with the soybean field expansion. However, Marcos was only distracted for a while reflecting how "this is a standard image of Mato Grosso, a rhea in the middle of soy ... an iconic image," and then he returned to talk about the human–machine labor changes. I interpreted this as a reflection of his preoccupation with a world where humans and machines are the key units that exist.

The rheas always stood out when we saw them, as there were almost no other animals or people to be seen in the vast fields. In the same landscape, we also saw some new chicken factory farms, which were utilizing the surrounding soybean and corn fields for feed. I asked details about the operations, and found out that the birds were cloned, and ready for butchering in 45 days. Two people were enough to take care of 20,000 birds, located in the long, low buildings shown in Figure 3.5.

While passing these installations in the car, we saw some dead wild animals lying on the roadsides. This roadkill included a large Amazonian tapir who laid in a spot where a small patch of forest remained. When Marcos saw these forest spots, he always wanted to emphasize that the region also had protection and space for animals. However, as far as I could see there were only very few small patches of forest here and there—mostly it was just endless plantations.

When answering the four key questions, it is essential to note not only what happens to individuals, species, and populations, but much more importantly, as the previous chapters discussed, to observe what happens to the relations of beings, to the diversity of existences, and their spectrum within the web of life. If possible, this should also include notes on the so-called more-than-human beings, in their wide spectrum. The way to access these broader existences typically requires living with locals who have a long-term understanding of what exists in

*Figure 3.5* Chicken production facilities in the middle of soybean plantations, south of Nova Mutum, near BR163, taken on November 19, 2019.
Source: Photo taken by the author.

that place, such as Indigenous people. Western or other scientists, who have succumbed to modernity and who arrive to the field with a positivist attitude, have very limited possibilities and epistemologies to be able to understand the fuller spectrum of what exists, or how to give it value.

The monocultural expansion and practices described above not only eradicate masses of existences, but they also redefine the relations of those species that remain in the locality with those that are introduced, which fundamentally alters the local web of life. For example, there are now plentiful, yet poisonous, crops that present a new and deadly food source to some of the local wildlife.

In addition to the interrelations, what exists in the place is also modified internally. An example of a more profound existential transformation is the genetic "enhancements," which are introduced by the scientific intervention of livestock breeders and those companies invested in expanding the monoculture. The bred varieties of chicken and other production animals are not the same as their wild or even domestic ancestors. They are transformed not only in how they can exist but also for how long, even if they treated better than in the livestock facilities. The role and importance of these species in and for the web of life has been transformed. Even the plant-based GM crops function as a biological contamination for non-GMO fields and varieties. Some GMOs, like the Bt-potato, are even classified as pesticides, as the genetic modification has inserted so much of the *Bacillus thuringiensis* (Bt) toxin that the potato is itself deadly when ingested by the Colorado potato beetle (Cummings 2008).

It is important to note that the actors operating under this logic only value specific and narrowly selected existences. Weis (2013) describes how the male chicks of layer chickens (those chickens that are genetically bred to lay eggs as efficiently and quickly as possible, rather than grow their flesh for meat) are deemed unnecessary. The male chicks are either chopped up alive, electrocuted, gassed, or thrown out as trash (literally stuffed alive into garbage bags where they will either suffocate or starve to death), as it is not economically worth it to keep them alive. The same goes for the male offspring of dairy cattle, which are killed at a young age. These individuals are kept alive in extreme confinement (to make sure minimal movement) with nutritionally deficient diets to produce no-fat, anemic meat. In practice, the "producers," as they call themselves, see these beings solely as meat, from the beginning, and not as existing beings. This monoculturization of existences continues throughout the commodity chain, from plantations to factory farms with strict constraints on what species are able to exist, and in which form.

In summary, the agroextractivist expansion in northern Mato Grosso has changed very large areas of the Cerrado-Amazon forests into the type of agribusiness distribution and spectrum of life described above. This configuration of the web of life radically delimits the possibilities of what is allowed to exist there. The forms of life that exist there now are mostly cloned and GM varieties of soybean, corn, and cotton. A few humans also live there, including the owners and operators of the plantations and their workers, but their numbers are diminishing due to rapid automatization of machineries. There are still some wild animals, like the rheas, which can partially co-exist with the plantations. In addition, there are the pests and weeds, whose numbers and variety are constantly increasing if new agrotoxics—in larger and larger quantities—are not regularly spread on the fields to poison and kill them. Finally, there are some industrial chicken farms that exist in the area, with their minimal human workers and millions of cloned chickens for meat production. Otherwise, there is not much else that exists in the area, or is even given the possibility to be born and live out their existence in the area. This is a huge difference compared to the pre-extractivist Cerrado and Amazon forest worlds with their rich multitude of different life-forms and living beings. The Amazon is estimated to have "over three million species, and over 2,500 tree species" (Thomson 2020). It is especially worrying that in the Cerrado the species richness and endemism are highest in the highlands targeted by plantation expansion, this deforestation having led to an imminent "extinction risk of Cerrado endemic species" (Colli, Vieira, and Dianese 2020, 1470).

This region was very different before the forests were overridden by the soybean plantations. The Cerrado, is the high plain of South America where many of its biggest rivers start, and it has a very unique and magical feeling, which goes beyond raw numbers or taxonomic distinctions of the plants and animals. I know this feeling through my own experience of having traveled across different South American regions. In 2018, I traveled for the first time to the wonderful national parks and waterfall-rich forests a few hours to the north and west of Brazil's capital city, Brasília. My travel companions and I felt astonished by the feeling of this incredibly beautiful and serene plateau. Many people have noted this before, and for many human groups, the Cerrado is a specifically sacred area. For example, there are hundreds of different religions or spiritual organizations that have meditation or other types of spiritual centers established around the National Park of Chapado dos Veadeiros. There is much more to existence than just the numbers or names of species, and in answering the four key questions on existences, it is important not to be stuck to the conventions of Western science, or what is now known to science, but to also venture beyond. The array of what exists is wide and uncountable. To get an idea of the magic of Cerrado, which goes beyond words, I recommend taking a look at the art created by artists living in the region, such as Cris Maia, Marcos Brasil, and Wagner Maia from the Atelier Preguiça, whose work is inspired by immersion in the nature of Cerrado.[2]

## How they can exist (what is the quality of existence)?

The second key question is important to ask as it focuses attention on the following aspects of existence:

- How do the beings exist in a given area?
- What is the quality of their existence?
- Do they suffer, or is their existence happy, for the time that they exist?
- How has the quality of existence changed with the expansion of extractivism?

I will start to answer these questions by looking at the existences of the chickens that we encountered, who live their whole lives in industrial feedlot facilities. In these industrial livestock factories, the bodies and the existence of the animals is so skewed that there is little to no other possibility left for how those species and beings would otherwise behave or live. The biological rhythm of the animals is changed because the lamps are lit all the time, so they have no sense of day or night. The living space of the animals is extremely limited, so if they can even move within their enclosure it is an extremely minimal movement. The metabolism of the animals is modified, and they have also been denied normal sexual behavior and are unable to raise their offspring. In short, meat extractivism currently operates through the existential transformation of the beings themselves. As Weis (2013, 112) describes:

> The transformation of bodies is so radical that copulation is physically impossible for genetically enhanced turkeys, nearly impossible for broiler chickens, and increasingly difficult for pigs. Specialized breeding populations are also necessitated by the fact that most of their offspring are killed before reaching sexual maturity.

This violence has turned the whole existence of these beings into a monotonous life. The analysis by Weis (2013, 141) opens up the miserable quality of these lives:

> Environments of concrete and steel lead to extreme sensory deprivation and monotony. Animals are cut off from daily and seasonal rhythms and the ability to breathe fresh air, play, explore, or find food, sun, or shade, and are faced with frustrated co-inhabitants instead of families, social groups, and playmates. The collective 'stress' and ill-health are acknowledged only to the extent that they impair production, and are then overridden in a variety of ways, including through routine, unanesthetized bodily mutilations.

Besides the miserable lives of factory farm animals, there are other animal lives that are deeply affected by the extension of the monoculture. For example, some wild animals have gained more food to eat because of corn plantations, but research has shown that this food source has caused health problems, as the corn and soybeans are heavily poisoned. In addition, the animals that cause noticeable losses to the crops are killed with poison or by other means. It is also quite clear that the insects and other animals, who are targeted by agrotoxics, cannot be described as having a good quality of life when they get killed as the way the poisons kill these beings is not what would be considered a normal or natural death for them. The operational mechanisms of the poisons negatively affect the nervous system. These agents were discovered during the Second World War and were used to produce nerve gas. After that war ended, another war continued, in the fields affected by the so-called Green Revolution (see Patel 2009).

In addition to the effects on the other-than-humans, the humans living in the area were also impacted by the poisoning and other harmful aspects of the agribusiness. The salaries seemed to be normal for the manual workers in this area, so the key problem here did not turn on the amount of money paid to workers, or being forced to work in slave-like conditions, as in many ranches in Brazil.[3] Yet, the work was monotonous and the hours long. In addition, the extractivist capitalists living in the area seemed to be extremely busy, mostly thinking about work and increasing production, as they were constantly pressured by the necessity to expand and take bigger loans. They were also increasingly worried by rising climate disruptions. To understand how the soybean producers experienced the quality of life in the region now, in comparison to the past, I asked Marcos, "And what is life now like, with the people who are here?" He replied with a happy, satisfied face, being proud of the region:

> Ah, it improved a lot, a lot of people came here, and this opened a lot of opportunities for industry, agriculture, professionals, agronomy, the quality of life is good, maybe. . .here you don't have all the entertainment you have in the big center, but here you don't have the social problems you have in big cities, you don't have a periphery here, everyone has a job, the region is prosperous because of this.

He also argued that there is a lack of qualified workers, and I asked where they come from, to help understand what kind of people live in the region. He argued that most of these people come from abroad, that they "come from the United States," to install ethanol facilities as technicians. In response to my questions about the worker salaries, he told me that a machine operator would gain on average between 4,000 and 5,000 BLR (862–1,077 euros) per month, or at least four minimum salaries, and that they have very few living costs as they live free on properties and do not pay taxes. He indicated that he has 20 workers to maintain his operations.

The number of people who benefit from the agribusiness model as workers is extremely limited, when considering the hectares that need to be occupied by plantations for the creation of just one job. The jobs people have and that they can have in an area, are relational. Jobs need to be examined in relation to the effects on other jobs and quality of lives of others living in the area, including the general possibilities to have a job. While agribusiness has expanded, the number of people living in the countryside has seen a dramatic decline, which has led to a rural exodus to city favelas, and landless camps in the countryside (Oliveira and Hecht 2016). This process has benefited only a very small number of professionals and elites, due to which Ioris (2017), drawing especially on Mato Grosso's soybean expansion, calls Brazil's dominant agricultural system agro-neoliberalism. The peasants and traditional communities, who are allowed to stay in the broader area, are pushed to live on the margins of the soybean production and protected areas. However, even the protected areas are experiencing worsening conditions—directly and indirectly—due to the overall impact of soybean expansion (Eloy et al. 2016).

Marco's reference to the most skilled workers coming from the United States is quite revealing. These areas are retained principally for a small slice of American, European, and, more recently Chinese extractivist corporations and their employees. Brazil's soybean plantations are enclaves for the foreign corporations, Brazilian agribusiness, and their model of land use. These entities define who is able to make earnings based on their operating model. These powerhouses also define who has the right to exist, who can exist, and even how they exist in the area.

The few workers hired for agroextractivist soybean operations on the large plantations of Brazil's North and Center-West regions are skilled workers, who come mostly from the South, and not the local unskilled, rural people (Garrett and Rausch 2016). Furthermore, these agribusiness workers, as discussed previously, are under a constant threat of losing their jobs, as automation is expanding. Their current lives, as workers without sufficient protections within the constantly poisoned fields, may have a good quality for a while, but eventually, many of them are prone to experience a worsening quality of life due to repeated exposure to agrotoxics. Nevertheless, in comparison to all other living beings now residing in these extractivist enclaves, such as the broiler chickens or insects, the humans who are allowed to remain there, can be justifiably seen as having a wonderful quality of life.

Comparison of this arrangement of existences with the situation prior to the expansion of the monocultures suggests an abysmal worsening of living conditions for most species and beings. In the ruins of post-extraction landscapes, once the "resources" have run out, what remains is machineries, waste, and barren landscapes. These modern infrastructures cause pain and despair to the people who must live in their midst (Truscello 2020). This is the answer to the question "what" exists after extractivist expansions, especially in the cases when extraction is allowed to continue until there is nothing left to extract.

## In which time and/or how long can they exist?

There are several dimensions carried by this third, temporal question in the study of existences:

- How long can the beings present exist, when extractivism continues?
- Has the lifespan of different species increased or decreased?
- What has happened to the way time is experienced?
- How have the conceptions of time changed?

I will answer these questions by continuing to focus on the expanding agroextractivism and monoculturization in northern Mato Grosso.

How long a certain species can exist is redefined when monocultures replace whatever existed in the area before (such as a forest) with a very limited array of existences. Agroextractivist plantations result in a fast-life cycle, as generally the cloned plant or tree is only intended to live a few years of existence (if that even). These new accelerated existences are forced to stand on top of land that used to host a species-rich forest with many varying lifespans, as time treats various plants or trees very differently. In fact, asking this third time-related key question opens up several important onto-epistemological questions on temporality, and how to study the temporal transformations related to major landscape changes. The conception or understanding of time within modernity is linear, which could be described as sequential or a series of events that happen in a particular order and lead in a particular direction. However, there are many other cosmologies, ontologies (Blaser, 2013), and states of being that have different conceptions of time. As Gan et al. (2017, 10) emphasize, modernity's "metronomic synchrony is not the only time that matters." With that in mind, extractivisms have an impact not only on how long a species can exist (in the modern era) but they also rearrange conceptions of time. This is an important point with respect to averting the risk of reification of modernist worldviews inherent to environmental economics that focuses on calculating the value of existences (e.g., number, type, and length) through established biological lenses and norms of valuation.

In the post-frontier space of soybean plantations, time flows following the order of commodity production. That is, time is compelled along in a machine-like rhythm, continually running faster to keep pace with the demands to quicken the process of monotonous time. This is done by increasing the number of harvests per year, increasing the number of truckloads transported, growing the chickens faster to produce more meat and slaughter them even faster by setting targets for workers to reach certain number of beheadings per shift. Now compare this temporal space for existence in those spaces with the multitude of factors beyond this productivist drive, including the ontological multiplicity of the beings, socioenvironmental processes (such as Indigenous agroforestry or hunting and collecting cycles), ecological processes (such as soil microbes transforming soils), and everything else that is beyond the modern worldview in the pluriverse (all such relations, aspects, and entities to which Indigenous and other forest-dwellers and traditional peoples and communities refer to and include in their ontologies).[4] There is an existential divide between these processes, which also divides time; it divides how time runs for beings, some of which might be the same individuals before and after the frontier expansion. The notion of "frontier" is again useful here, as framed in the film *Dances with the Wolves*. Once the main character arrives to the frontier of the American conquest and the Indigenous groups, the way time starts to run for him changes, as well as the Indigenous people being hunted by the colonizers. Many of the people who have to face such expansions of extractivist frontiers around the world are either killed, or, if they survive they have to change their occupations, to work for the extractivists, e.g., as butchers in slaughterhouses or gold diggers. This also changes the conceptions of time, and so much more. The altered array of existences and lived environments continues to reproduce miserable lives even after the extraction.

The third sub-question of how long the process seems to continue, and are there transformations that change existences, is important for considering how long this existence changing process can continue to exist. Is this a self-destructive process? What will come after? Significant parts of the deforested Amazon forests have been revegetated by secondary forests, after predominantly pasture or logging areas are left outside of extractivist uses (see Fearnside 2008). However, this is far less likely for the agroextractivist monoculture areas, primarily because, in comparison to pastures and logging, it is very difficult for native vegetation and forests to expand in the heavily poisoned and eroded soils. Second, these areas are incorporated into a wider system, and are more deeply embedded in the logic and chains of extraction.

How long can this extraction continue? The history of the transatlantic is full of stories of how the expansion of monocultures, how the extraction of wood deforested entire islands and regions, and how the extensive use of land for sugarcane and other plantations caused erosion and the need to move to new areas (Moore 2015; Perlin 2005). Currently, more emphasis is laid on trying to use other means, via capital intensification, to avoid the need to simply expand to new localities to maintain agricultural productivity, e.g., through the expansion of some form of "agroforestry," like planting some trees in the midst of plantations (Ollinaho and Kröger 2021). However, these are not real long-term solutions. Ioris (2017), drawing on the Mato Grosso soybean frontier's actual impacts, suggests that the agro-neoliberal model of Brazil seems to be headed toward the same destiny as the Titanic. The Titanic was heralded as a marvel and framed the most modern ship of its time. One could have full confidence of capacities and capabilities, and there is no need to be afraid of or respect natural conditions of the sea it traveled on. There are many similarities with this modernist supremacy idea that are replicated through the agribusiness model. This extractivist expansion has already hit its own iceberg, and is sinking, while desperate means are taken to fix the widening holes in the system. The current agroextractivist-feed-livestock complex cannot continue its existence in the current form of production, but must try increasingly desperate means to overcome developing pest resilience and diseases of monoculturally grown animals and crops. Typically, these means signify ever deeper and harmful, depleting impacts, in a much longer time frame. While the sinking of the Titanic caused death when it sank, it was only able to sink once. The sinking extractivist model will continue to cause deaths even after its demise, due to the pollutants it leaves behind. As Weisman (2007) describes in *The World Without Us,* the pesticides created by the agrochemical industry contain some of the world's most complex molecules, which are likely to persist the longest of all current, human-created artifacts, as nature does not yet know how to dispose of them through disintegration or decomposition. The logic, described by Weis (2013, 126) for crops and animal farms, trying to continue cheap production, is destructive in itself:

> As with monocultures, contradictions are never resolved but are instead overridden at every turn. Overrides involve varying combinations of antibiotics, vaccines, hormones, insecticides, disinfectants, artificial inseminators, physical mutilations, heating, lighting, ventilation systems, large volumes of - water, slurry

pumps, sprayers, and lagoons, along with the energy needed to transport things over greater distances.

When reading the above passage through the approach I am suggesting in this book, the reference to "overrides" can be understood as referring to killings in general, the eradication of lives. It references a violent, suffocating aversive logic, which leads to far worse problems, such as pandemics. Within this logic, as time passes, and violent actions deepen, even by the supposed corrective measures taken according to the business-as-usual mentality, the war against life deepens and expands. This war against life is not a cold war, but a hot war that is constantly getting hotter. At some point, however, fires, pandemics, droughts, storms, and other, unexpected yet already foreseen events, may force even this logic to change, or to self-destruct. Weis (2013) sees that most of the above problems stem from the logic of standardizing the species and production methods. Thus, an antidote to agroextractivism would be to focus resistance attempts on diversifying existences, of crops, animals, and all other beings, not uniting them under a singular logic, which radically limits what can exist. This is exactly what movements, such as La Via Campesina and several food sovereignty movements have called for, in their defense of their traditional cultivation methods and plants (Patel 2009).

Times are changing with the global crises, such as the climate emergency. I asked Marcos if the locals think of climate change, and what will happen to this region. To my surprise, he explained that they are already seeing and somewhat worried about climate and ecological changes, "We have to understand that in a little while it can change, reduce the rains, that's why there are many places that are already having irrigation, but I think that irrigation can also be a way to end the water springs…I do not know." Climate scholars argue that the Amazon may have already reached a tipping point, whereafter much of the Amazon will turn to savannahs, in an irreversible process, or at least it is currently at this threshold (Lovejoy and Nobre 2019). This would signify much faster advancing fires, loss of essential rains, and other problems, such as uncontrollable pests. All of these trends, considered in the larger context of runaway increases of global emissions, suggest that the times of agroextractivism may come to an end in Mato Grosso sooner rather than later. What will come after this rhythm of monocultural existences remains unknown. An even deeper extractivism? A post-extractivist landscape? Based on a political-economic analysis, I think it is unlikely that the current power holders in this area would allow the region to take a radically different direction. This region is currently regarded as a playground whose production parameters, what to produce and for whom, are designated and orchestrated by a few global, national, and regional agribusiness corporations.

In summary, those plants and farm animals who currently exist in plantation monocultures have very short lives and life cycles, which are continually replaced with equally bleak existences by the fast-production cycle. Most insects and many wild animals' lives also come to an end too soon. Humans have also experienced a transition and live according to a time where they carry the sensation that time is running ever faster and to survive one needs to constantly battle and develop. This is a radically distinct, extractivist time conception, in comparison to the understanding of time that the Indigenous populations in the area had prior to the arrival of European settlers' and their conception of time. This change in terms of time is at least as noted and radical as the decrease in the spectrum and quality of life. Yet, for many Indigenous groups, time is not linear, but circular (Rifkin 2017), as such Indigenous temporalities work as an antidote to the extractivist logic and practices developing among them.

## Who are the key entities deciding and contesting the rights to exist?

This fourth question directs the attention toward assessing in more detail the politics around the other three existential questions of how an activity like extractivism can transform existences. It is useful here to note the role of both social actors, such as different company, government, state, and non-governmental organizations, social movements, and human groups, as well as the key individual actors within them. Here, one can also add the voices of other-than-human actors, as represented by humans, in the way proposed by Political Ontology (Blaser 2009; de la Cadena 2015).

For this fourth question, I do not mean making a "stakeholder" analysis, or even just surveying the politics between different actors. Instead, the focus is on existential politics. This question directs attention to who has the power to decide what can live in an area, and whose rights to exist are respected, ignored, or denied. When answering these questions, it helps to examine how the existences are transformed, and how extractivisms could be challenged. From ethnographic material, the points to pay attention to are the interviews or observed discourses and debates, which affect who can exist, and who is framed as not having the right, or given the right to exist in the area. One should make note of other existential political debates, discourses, and actions. It is also important to assess if and how varied existences are defended against ethno- and eco-cides. As with the first three questions, it is most useful to focus on the relations of different actors, and how these relations were before and how they are now, and how they have transformed through existential policy-making processes.

The key debates about Nova Mutum, and the process of deforesting the Cerrado–Amazon transition forests, revolve around different valuations given to what was there before, and what exists there now. The viewpoint of soybean producers differed dramatically from the viewpoint of other actors, such as Indigenous groups and their representatives. Soybean producers, as they called themselves, were the most important actors deciding what has value, and what can live and what does live in this region. When I was asking Marcos about the deforestation of the region, he asked me:

> I ask you what that vegetation from before [referring to the area he had deforested from its natural state] produced? It was a crooked wood Cerrado, [which] produced a lizard and an armadillo, but today you still have these animals, on a smaller scale because he still lives there in that forest, he eats this corn, if you go out there to the middle [pointing to the plantations] you will find his hole, armadillo, the bush pig that didn't exist [here before] it now comes to eat and has enough [food for himself]. So, we are living a balance, we have some losses [in the crops] sometimes with these pigs and these rheas, we will not kill them to see them die, there are tapirs if you come one day with time and walk in these woods you see a lot of animals, tapir, collared peccary, rhea, seriemas, deer, and armadillo.

Of notable importance in the above discourse is the pejorative reference to the Cerrado as producing just armadillos and lizards, and having crooked woods that he did not consider to be real forests. The key point of valuation, the unit of value creation and division, seems to be production; that is, who produces and who does not produce. It is important to note the attempt to downplay the diversity and importance of what existed in the deforested areas. Such framing attempts were constant during the visits I had to the plantations with their controllers. There seemed to be the feeling that the farmers needed to justify their past actions by such framings, which amounted to imagining that the current situation would mean living in "balance."

Researchers are a key group who contest the claims of agroextractivists on what exists and how. Scientific studies seem to negate many of the factual claims made by the soy producers about the impacts of their actions. This is seen especially clearly when a challenge is made to the point about the situation being in balance. Rekow (2019, 8) argues that "large-scale production of soy is associated with loss, deterioration and changes in the Cerrado's biophysical foundations. It negatively impacts on native vegetation, soil, groundwater, hydrological patterns, and other elements essential to socio-ecological security." In fact, such imbalance is clearly visible to any outsider who is not used to seeing endless soybean fields, and who understands what kind of forest used to be in the same place before the soybeans came. The imbalance is so great, that researchers are calling for extending the Amazon soy moratorium to the Cerrado, as the current pace of deforestation will end up putting—ironically—the existing plantation activities at risk.[5] The below excerpt from Soterroni et al. (2019, 4) illustrates the typical reference to the importance of undisturbed Cerrado, of which less than 20 percent remains:

> The Cerrado is a global biodiversity hot spot and provides essential ecosystem services for Brazil, including the provision of water, agricultural products, and carbon sequestration....The Amazon and the Cerrado also provide direct regulation of the regional climate via transpiration, which is the source of most of the regional rainfall—the water source that soybeans and other crops depend upon in this rain-fed agricultural system.

Research on the environmental damage caused by soybean plantations tells a story of imbalance, especially via the rapidly increasing and worsening use of agrotoxics. Northern Mato Grosso is the region of Brazil where the most agrotoxics are used. Medici et al. (2021, 1) found pesticides and metals in Cerrado tapirs that exceed safe levels and raise concern for adverse health impacts, arguing that "Brazil is one of the biggest consumers of pesticides in the world and allows the use of chemicals that are banned in many other countries due to their adverse health effects in a wide range of species, including humans."

The key debates also revolve around trying to compare the current situation at the point of extraction to an even worse situation elsewhere. Marcos Ioris wanted to emphasize that his plantations and actions in Nova Mutum were much more sustainable and within the current law than the deforesting and criminal activities in the Pará state in the Amazon. He argued that he was against the idea of turning the Amazon forests into plantations. Instead, he saw that the existing pastures should be used for extending plantations, to "make Brazil move forward," something that he thought Bolsonaro is starting to do. His vision for the Amazon was that:

> So, I think the Amazon has to be preserved offering conditions for the people who live there. The Indigenous people have to live in their reserve and explore it ecologically with sustainability, the riverside dwellers have to live of fishing and of the extraction of açai berry, guarana, cocoa, and Brazil nut, that are found there too, they need to have the means for this to happen. These people are there, and they might not wish to live like this anymore, to be forced to live like that.[6] The forest is rich, I think the state of Pará disappointed since the territory was battered with livestock, today you can no longer explore that much. It is necessary to regulate, to create means for those people. Back in the 70s there was an incentive to go to the Amazon and there are people who did it, but could not do anything until today, because the forest is thick, the resources are scarce, and the roads are bad. So, I believe there must be a balance. I'm not against the world coming here in Brazil and saying that we have to preserve the Amazon. I'm not against it but you have to create means for the people there to be able to live and support themselves.

Yet, although Marcos wanted to distance the impact of his soybean plantations on the Amazon deforestation, studies show that the expansion of soybeans onto pastures is the trigger process that drives ranchers further into the Amazon. This highlights the extent to which one needs to observe the inter-regional dynamics of frontier processes when considering existential redistributions (see Kröger and Nygren 2020). Singular area studies are not enough to understand the cascading impacts on existences that interlinked commodity frontiers have. Also, it is essential not to downplay the value of life in areas such as the Cerrado and the borders of the Amazon, by considering the Cerrado as a non-forest area with "nothing" (as Marcos argued several times in the above quotes). In reality, Cerrado, as Luis Carlos Sampaio from the Kabu Institute of the Kayapó Indians argued (interview, Novo Progresso, November 20, 2019), has been unfortunately forgotten due to its location next to the Amazon, which has received almost all of the attention of those concerned about deforestation, including environmentalists. He had been living and working for several decades with many different Indigenous people of the Amazon and the Cerrado, and reflected on what he had learned. While standing by a beautiful riverside near Novo Progresso, he replied to my question on what the Cerrado is and has, in terms of life, in the following way:

> … the Cerrado is our forest turned upside down, right? The roots are deep, there is not much water, right? An incredible diversity of plants, and it is almost disappearing, you see? There where you [still] have Cerrado [left] today there are Indigenous areas, units of conservation, right, which have areas of Cerrado. The Kaiapó used to live in the Cerrado in the past. It was afterwards that they came to the [Amazon] forest. They say that there are lot of plants, lot of medicines, lots of fruits. And this is true. The Cerrado is rich. I worked with the Bakairi, with the Bakairi Indians, who live there in open Cerrado. They were [always] bringing a lot of fruits…

The producer associations and their largest landholders hold the key power in deciding what can exist in the agroextractivist areas, and what changes are made in terms of existences. There are two different associations of rural producers in Nova Mutum, one for corn and soybean producers, who have the same chain of production, while the other is for cotton producers, who normally must have at least 100,000 hectares of land. These bigger producers have a key role, while the others conform and follow their decisions in Mato Grosso, as this is the developmental path that is offered to them. For example, the Maggi family members have huge land holdings and plantations in the state, over one-million-hectares according to my informants. Blairo Maggi has been Brazil's Minister of Agriculture and the governor of Mato Grosso, and he is the key owner of the influential agribusiness corporation Amaggi. These interlinked politician-agroextractivists are the key decision makers, and, according to Marcos Ioris, the key task of the rural associations is to ensure the producers voices are heard among them, the task of the associations being principally to, "try to bridge the political part, the government part, with the producer, the producer's needs, the discussions there in Brasília, with the deputy, when they want to increase the tax rate, we go in there and start making our own defenses, our claims."

I saw how this agricultural lobby works in practice by making observations in the congress in Brasília, by attending meetings and commissions where topics of interest to agroextractivists were discussed. The continual growth of the power and lobbying capacities of agribusiness are widely recognized as the key explanations of Brazilian politics and deepening socio-ecological problems (e.g., de Area Leão Pereira et al. 2020; Dowbor 2019; Ioris 2017; Kröger 2012, 2017; Souza 2019).

The agribusiness lobby and its congressional counter-part, the Rural Caucus (officially called *Frente Parlamentar da Agropecuária* or FPA), are the main explanation for Brazil being such a key place for expanding monocultures and allowing for agrotoxics in greater number and quantity in spite of the global ecological crises. The FPA is widely funded by multinational and national agribusiness, the feed trade, agrotoxic producers, and meat corporations, such as Cargill, Bayer, Basf, BRF, JBS, Syngenta, and Bunge, as well as banks like Santander (Arroyo, 2020).

The workers in Nova Mutum were practically non-organized, even their training was organized by a syndicate of the large producers and not by a rural workers' trade union. According to Marcos, the existing rural syndicate is "of the producers, but focused on training the worker, the union belongs to the producer, I am a member, I pay a monthly fee, we have courses for tractor operator, canteen worker, cleaning lady, harvester operator, planter..." Thus, it seems that in this area there are no relevant rural workers' associations, such as the Brazilian Landless Movement or rural trade unions, contesting what is happening.

Environmental officers also have a say, according to the producers, as they have put some farms on hold or forbidden them to cultivate due to infractions of environmental obligations, especially for deforesting too extensively. Due to the pressure for environmental protection, there is a new surge in the demand to show that one has protected the required amount of land. However, the way this is done has been distorted to the benefit of the farmers. The current logic of protection illustrates how an extractivist logic has penetrated even the conservation efforts of private properties in Brazil. There is a surge in the land market because of the new requirements, which dictate that one must be able to show that a certain percentage of their lands have been preserved. This market of ecological compensation functions through the following logic, which Marcos further explained:

> In practice I go to the environmental agency, to regularize my area, and he says that I deforested there x hectares, then I look at the plan, the PRA, the regularization program, then they give me a deadline, and sometimes they even indicate me some areas too, or I look for friends, neighbors, or someone who has an area that is just bush and wants a part [of the profits in the compensation scheme], then you negotiate, get that registration there and document it with your area [linking the productive and protected areas]. I have an area of 250 hectares, for example, which is all

> overgrown, which is not here on this property. [With that area], I can do this [sell the preservation status of the land in the compensation market] or hold it for myself, [for me] to open another piece in the future and register that [piece of land as the preserved part].

It is interesting to note in the above passage the pejorative references given to forests—"bush" and "overgrown"—as these are signs of an attempt to delegitimize their existences and right to exist. Yet, as these areas are given some new value in the 2012 Forest Code, which in general worsened the possibilities and need to protect forests, besides introducing demands for compensation in a market-based logic (Kröger 2017), these forests that need to be protected have been inserted within the logic of the producers. This logic revolves around profit, markets, business, and trading—not around protection, as it should. This can be seen from the references in the above passage to trading the rights to deforest due to having protected another area. This is telling of the dangers of ecological compensation schemes. In terms of existential politics, these legislations or policies seem to feed the problematic logic that is the premise for most modern business, which is the flattening and denial of existences, at the cost of making them tradable commodities.[7] These compensation schemes have the assumption that one life can be compensated with another life, which reflects the mass-like ontology of biodiversity and many biological studies and approaches. There is the idea that a destroyed spectrum of existence could be compensated by archiving a slice of it in some other place. This is a fallacy. As de la Cadena (2020) argues, water is not the same water everywhere. If one destroys 5,000 hectares of forest, the life there does not relocate to another protected area, nor is it compensated in any such way. This is because the destroyed trees in that place are not the same trees as in the other place. This kind of approach is essential in bringing forth a new viewpoint to counter the growing tendency to expand ecological compensation schemes, which are based on an understanding of life as ecosystem activities and biodiversity analysis. There are many more pitfalls than promises in such false solutions, and they should be avoided. These schemes seem to be working for the benefit of further extractivist expansions.

Legal experts are very worried about these developments in Brazil, which are linked to the overall tendency of using laws and lawmaking to advance corrupted political aims, through what could be termed "lawfare," instead of trying to create a rule of law that would apply equally to all. The role of the judiciary, judicial politics, and lawyers has increased in Brazil since the 2010s, as key elected politicians have been sidelined by the growing power of prosecutors and judges. Even the soy producers need to utilize specialists to work through legal settings. Many of these legal maneuvers are done to please the foreign observers, in an attempt to make the operations appear as though they are working. These legal politics are hugely impacted by the demand of foreign commodity buyers and consumers. However, in practice, many of these market-led legal interventions into policies are not effective and ultimately end up creating new problems. When taking existences into account, the ecological compensation policies, whose intentions were framed as good and suited to protect nature, seem to have created major problems. Patricia Silva, a legal expert I interviewed in Brasília, at the premises of the Brazilian Congress in early November 2019, explained to me the impacts that the 2012 new Forest Code and its compensation policies have had for regions such as Nova Mutum:

> It's what I call Green *Grilagem* [theft of land by falsifying land deeds], large areas that will be totally homogeneous, just soybeans, because there will be no connectivity between the forests, which would be the role of the legal reserves, to establish gene flow of the forest. . .[and] guarantee water—she [water] ends up, do you understand Markus, the properties all transformed into just soy; and this is the end. And his legal reserve is in another state [of Brazil], this is what is allowed now.

The key actors who decide what can exist and how it can exist in Nova Mutum, are those who have incorporated, operate through, live their daily lives, and act within the capitalist and extractivist logic, where the calculation of profits and costs occupies a key role in thinking. The soybean producers were immersed in such thinking, where the imperatives and contours flowed from the global and national political economy of producing cheap commodities for feedlots. Instead of thinking about how their lifestyles and daily actions affect who and what can exist, the minds of the producers seemed to be deeply involved in profit-making and cost structure calculations within the markets where they lived. These markets seemed to be distanced and abstracted from the reality of the existences on the ground. Marcos discussed the cost structure of soybean operations, explaining that "about 65 percent of the cost of the crop goes to fertilizer, seed, diesel oil, salaries of labor, and defensives." The rest of the costs, which do not reach 100 percent, but at maximum a total of 80 percent, 20 percent being the minimum accepted profit, consists of "taxes, freight, and the maintenance of machines." The agrotoxics, seeds, and fertilizers are the single most expensive cost categories, fertilizers being 40 percent of these three items, as it must almost all be bought with dollars, as it is imported. I asked how much he produces and gains profit per hectare, and he estimated that he produces on average 60 bags of soybeans per hectare, gaining approximately 1,200 dollars in revenue, the costs of production being 1,000 dollars per hectare. On top of this 200-dollar profit per hectare for soybeans come the possible yields from the corn that is the next crop planted in the succession. This shows how there is definitely an extractivist and capitalist logic and practice present, which is centered around producing cheap commodities for global production, and making profits so large that these processes were certainly going to continue expanding, if the material conditions allowed.

This same market logic was pervasive in the town of Nova Mutum. There did not seem to be any notable resistance actors, environmental, or other NGOs operating there. Life revolved very much—almost solely—around the task of producing soybeans, corn, and cotton commodities in masses, and as cheaply as possible.

When considering the politics of existences, it is also important to make notes on the role and power that the extractivist technologies and established infrastructures have. Once these have been established, some of them start to live their own lives. Some scholars refer to, in a Latourian sense, the toxic "lagoons" created by mines, as things, which have agency (e.g., Li 2015).[8] The existence of these and other new extractivist things does affect power relations, and thus also what kind of politics, and policy changes, are possible and feasible. The usage of glyphosate, as a political- economic action and technological tool, has become very much locked-into industrial agriculture (Clapp 2021). The vast plantations I saw in Mato Grosso, and their growing use of pesticides, attest to this. The combination of GM seeds, glyphosate, and no-tilling machines function as a technological lock-in, whose result is the consolidation and concentration of power and land control. The breeding animals and crops are controlled by a diminishing number of actors (Weis 2013). Expanding these agroextractivist monocultures is a way to center power and control, in a way that is much more radical and physically-rooted than power measures taking place mostly in the social or symbolic spaces (see Kröger 2016a).

Once regions are transformed into dedicated agroextractivist or mining extractivist sites, they are hard to transform to other uses. Yet, they will remain as centers of power within broader global chains, and later they will be abandoned as they are now spaces of degradation and ruination. It will be harder to cast these areas off their designated role as enclaves for the particular slice of the global extractivist complex that has transformed the area beyond recognition and often beyond the possibilities of repair and reform. This is, in my view, a key explanation for why soybeans, and not some other commodities, such as oil palm, are planted in such an extensive way in Brazil. Once that particular agroextractivist system gets rooted to a certain point, it gets a hold of the lands, and starts to copy and expand itself, and the interests of those gaining from this expansion just grow. Based on their grip on these enclaves, the producers, traders, and processors can create extremely cheaply produced consumer commodities, and gain extraordinary profits. These profits further consolidate the grip of the system, thus propagating its continued expansion. The infrastructural and technological "developments" that ensue, are produced within this extension, not only to allow, but to lock-in the kind of land uses that benefit these actors. This is not a rational process, in which the most productive or sound options would be produced on a piece of land. Capitalism does not seem to operate through such rationality. There is no invisible hand directing the best possible production to where it is best to produce those goods. Instead, political-economic groups and sectors that become regionally dominant, are a much sounder explanation for who and what can exist in a given area.

Given the types of social actor settings described, wherein power is heavily skewed towards the agroextractivist producers, it is understandable why and how only certain existences are valued via the daily practices of monocultural operations, while most rights to exist are not recognized, seen, or are outright denied. These monocultural logics also operate at the global level, following the soybean complex. I will next make some concluding remarks on these cascading effects of the monocultural and extractivist logics.

## Notes

1. I would recommend further reflection on the kind of infrastructures that are expanded via extractivisms, and for the purpose of greater extraction within a global commodity production (Arboleda 2020; Bunker and Ciccantell 2006), which has violent characteristics (Dunlap and Jakobsen 2020) that amount to a brutal necropolitics, which deny existences via expanding toxicity and death (Truscello 2020).
2. https://www.ateliepreguica.com.br/
3. Between 1995 and 2000, over 55,000 people who were working in conditions analogous to slavery were liberated in Brazil, where contemporary slavers are a serious problem, violating the rights of especially young illiterate rural men. https://escravonempensar.org.br/o-trabalho-escravo-no-brasil/ (accessed March 23, 2021)

4. Traditional Peoples and Communities is an official category, which has been given specific territorial rights by the Brazilian state based on their long-term habitation or livelihood, such as rubber tapping, collecting nuts, or artisanal fishing. In many cases they live very similarly to Indigenous people, and they can also include Indigenous, Afro-Brazilian Quilombo communities, and people within the territories to which they have been given communal rights. Currently, all these peoples are under severe threat and are being targeted by Bolsonaro's regime (Margutti, de Pinho, and Oliveira n.d.).
5. The Amazon Soy Moratorium was launched in the late 2000s, after pressure from Greenpeace and others, where major soybean traders pledged not to buy soybeans from areas that were deforested after 2008. However, according to Lima et al. (2019), the execution of this policy has had serious limitations, as most cultivation has not been monitored by the moratorium, as revealed by a comparison to actual deforestation caused by soybeans.
6. The idea of Indigenous people being "forced" to live as they do is a common framing among Bolsonarists and large landholders in Brazil. They argue that the Indigenous people are forced to stay in poverty and misery, but would like to "develop," but are prohibited by NGOs and foreign powers, so that they or Brazil could not "develop." Bolsonaro argues that Indigenous people are used as agents in that way for foreign interests. For the current genocidal effects of these policies by Bolsonaro among Mato Grosso's Indigenous peoples, see Ioris (2020).
7. Polanyi's (2001) notes on fictitious commodities could be used and expanded for an analysis of the existential dynamics involved in the creation of such fictitious commodities of different types.
8. Haraway (2004) also has an expansive and broad scope when inquiring what exists, and questioning the current framings of who has the right to exist, or to speak for others. Future studies could delve deeper into the many potentialities in uniting the kind of analysis presented in this book with the multiple insights presented by Haraway (2004).

# 4 Conclusions

## Global extractivisms, the world-ecology, and existential redistributions

This book argues that the world's major extractivist expansions are accelerating, which causes annihilations and transformations that fundamentally redistribute existences, including who and what exists, and where and how they exist. This book explores many questions about existences in place and poses many questions around who is allowed to live and be born, how can they live, with what quality of life, for how long, and in which kind of time and rhythm of life? There is also a focus on who makes the decisions about such existential distributions, who imposes these decisions, and who contests them and how? How central to global extractivisms are the monocultural plantation model, racial, ethnic, and gender discriminations, ontological colonialism, and worker oppression? How do these dynamics relate to larger global changes? I will assess these questions from a broader perspective, reflecting on the current planetary moment.

A key starting point is to ask, what role do spaces of extraction play for global capitalism? How are existences redistributed when one observes the whole chain of causation—the commodity chain—from the fields, to the stomachs of production animals, to the consumers, and then to the waste yards? In this chapter, I will uncover some of the core dynamics related to global extractivisms and existential politics, and their wider links to the current world-system, beyond the contemporary focus that often turns on consumers or individuals. I also draw attention to how different forms of extractivist processes are based on assumptions of what beings and lives have value and which do not, and how these valuations and devaluations are actualized through existential annihilations and redistributions that reverberate throughout the global commodity chains.

DOI: 10.4324/9781003102977-5

## Global (agro)extractivisms

Global extractivism, as a concept, directs attention to the deeply material bases of capitalism and therefore the current world-system. The capitalist world-system needs to operate in an extractivist sense, to extract raw materials, for the continued functioning of several key industries, such as steel production. The extractivist mindset can even be seen in the metal and land acquisitions needed for so-called renewable energy transitions. Even the new economies of virtual worlds and information technology are inextricably based on this material reality, due to the energy and materials needed to run such operations. Despite this reality, there is the illusion that the world economy could be decoupled from its material impact on the earth. These ideas are normally presented by people, who have little understanding of the degree to which their decisions and consumer choices are dependent on daily extractions, both near and far.

Existential transformations caused by extractivist operations, such as monoculture expansions have cascading effects around the world, through their globalized production networks and value webs. Extractivisms, by their nature, re-create whole existential webs, in places far away from each other along the commodity chain. The case of soybean monoculture expansion, and the related global plant-feed-meat-laborer-consumer-waste chain, is an example of this. Soybean monocultures have led to vast and irreversible annihilations of the Cerrado and Amazon forests, including the life-forms, beings, and species that once formed the millions of hectares of forest, which were bulldozed and burned in just a handful of years to make way for this feed-production. The soybean feed is then transported to China and elsewhere, where factory farms of industrial pig and poultry production replicate the existential world of monocultural extractivism. Single species are selectively bred, only to live out their monotonous lives being fed by the monoculturally produced feed. Once they are killed, tens of thousands of similarly clothed workers cut the meat in monotonous routines. Consumers eat millions of units of similarly packed food products, and throw the waste out in landfills. The bones in these landfills are so numerous that they will remain a visible mark on the geological record (Patel and Moore 2017).

The agroextractivisms happening in places, such as the Cerrado and Amazon are important processes for global capitalist appropriation, but they are even more important in the current redistribution of global existences and the definition of what can exist, and how, around the world. Agroextractivisms have major influences throughout the commodity chain, and create global chains of existential redistributions. Thus, accumulation via agroextractivist expansion has major impacts on existences throughout the value webs of flex crops (see Borras et al. 2016) and webs of life (see Moore 2015), wherein the values of commodities are created. The analysis of existences in relation to agroextractivisms demonstrates how current capitalist value chains rely on reshaping existences and resisting any attempts to posit alternative, nonmonoculture existences. Essentially, political economic processes should be seen as existential processes.

The concept of an "industrial grain-oilseed-livestock complex" (Weis 2013, 8) is useful in highlighting and assessing the political economic system that leads to an equalization and unification of existences through a singular logic within the spheres where the system is dominant. Weis (2013, 8) explains how these widespread "islands of concentrated livestock and seas of monocultures" produce "heavy flows of crops, such as corn/maize," which are cycled through animals. This "disarticulation and rearticulation" is "mediated by an array of technologies, inputs, and large corporations, and marked by the loss of large volumes of usable nutrition" (Weis 2013, 8). To complement Weis's analysis, I would argue that the loss of "usable nutrition" could also be understood as the loss of countless lives through these processes. Of course, the loss of nutrition is fundamentally also a loss for those beings whose existences were based on the lost nutrition. Nutrition depletion, when seen through what exists in the soil, is also a loss of the lives and diversity of micro-organisms, and all the existences that create a living and healthy soil. This life can no longer be born and live where it would naturally due to the excessive extraction of so-called nutritional values, and the resulting erosion and depletion.

Besides nutrition, the diversity of existences is lost, both above and beneath the surface of the land. The depletion of the basic sustenance of life, at the root level, also signifies changes and existential losses along the whole chain of causation—the commodity chain.

The notion of the Plantationocene has surfaced to describe an era, which is dominantly characterized by the monotonizing and extractivist logic, which wreaks havoc in the form of extending industrial meat production and monoculture plantations over forests (Haraway 2015). Haraway et al. (2016) argue that the Plantationocene is a more apt term to describe the current epoch than Capitalocene (see Moore 2016), as the fundamental logic that explains the planetary shifts is the reordering or relocation of life that is essential to generate profits and capital. The reordered life Haraway talks about includes not only humans but also plants, microbes, animals, and other forms of life.

The plantation model disciplines people and plants alike, and operates especially by reordering time and forcing all kinds of forms of life to work for free or at a low cost (Mitman 2019). This argument is similar to my attempt with this book to direct more attention towardexistences, as a fundamental dimension that should be integrated into political economic, political ecological, and other analysis.

This plantation logic is not limited only to the Global South but also to extremely intensive farming practices in other places around the world. As Wolford (2021) emphasizes in her important article broadening the scope and scale of applying the Plantationocene concept, the former cores are currently seeing the rise of plantations, while factories settings have moved to the former peripheries, e.g., sweatshops. In Europe the situation is now worsened by the European Union's common agricultural policy (CAP), which drives intensive farming by rewarding the extent of cultivated land, rather than the quality of care given to the land. This accelerates environmental damages, as over 2,500 experts and several scientist associations have warned that the CAP is "turning rural areas into green deserts of uninhabitable maximum-yield monocultures" (Harvey 2019). Thus far appeals by scientists are rarely heeded, rather they are watered down by agribusiness lobbyists. Overall, the greatest problem is that extractivisms are in fact global. This global nature is very visible in the global food regime, where multinational corporations (mostly from Europe, the United States, and China) act destructively, e.g., by funding the Brazilian Rural Caucus, which is a large landholders' lobby group that controls the Brazilian parliament and its political economy (Arroyo 2020). More research needs to be directed—within the new research focus on plantations and the Plantationocene—to the resistance strategies that have managed to reverse and challenge the expansion of plantations, by documenting where and why this has happened, and by sharing the best practices with interested audiences. There are already such studies for different plantation sectors, which the current Plantationocene research can draw on to diversify its key message from one that is describing the problem to one that takes an emancipatory and practical approach to solving the problem. For example, there are important lessons provided in the book *Contentious Agency and Natural Resource Politics,* which are based on the resistance strategies working against the global expansion of tree plantations (Kröger 2013a). There are many existing pockets on the fringes of the Plantationocene debate, kind of side-products, where, e.g., Afrodescendant communities in the Atlantic world have centuries-old practices of agrobiodiversity and agroecology (Carney 2020). These communities could be shared as examples and as concrete, rooted localities from which to expand anti-extractivist actions to overcome the intersectionally discriminatory plantation economies.

## The expansion and limits of global extractivisms and existential redistributions

The chain of causation, in terms of existential reshufflings, runs both ways, causing pressures for further monotonization, control, and killings along commodity chains. These wreak havoc and change the way people and other beings exist, in terms of quality of life and the time that they live. It is important to note that global extractivisms, as they seek to produce cheap commodities, cause mass suffering to people and other beings all along the chain of extraction. This results in global existential shifts. Scholars of the rapidly expanded global meat system emphasize the continued deepening of class and ethnic inequalities (Winders and Ransom 2019). To be able to impose industrial livestock on a landscape, it is necessary that cheap resources also exist in that place—like cheap labor (Patel and Moore 2017), which can be exploited and coerced to work in the slaughterhouses. These slaughterhouses carry high health risks for workers (Isomäki 2021). In addition, this imposition of the globalized meat system is also largely based on exploiting ethnically marginalized people. For example, in the United States Latin Americans and African Americans make up the majority of workers in the poultry industry (Freshour 2019). Of the four key questions presented in this book, the question about the quality-of-life when taken to a global level of analysis, shows how the complete devaluation of animal lives is linked with a twisted logic that also devalues the people needed in the slaughterhouses and other types of labor as "a cheap and constant gendered and racialized workforce is as integral to global meat production as the acres of GMO feed or the selectively bred broilers" (Freshour 2019, 137). This is not new, but rather it is a basic feature of the Plantationocene expansion, which has been underway since the fifteenth century, and which Murphy and Schroering (2020) argue to be fundamentally based on the expansion of racial capitalism. The Plantationocene concept has been embraced recently in critical agrarian studies, political ecology, and agrarian studies, as it can offer more emphasis on the as-of-yet undernoted role of race and ethnicity, and the centrality of the plantation logic in many areas of the so-called modern world (Wolford 2021).

The key mechanism of extractivist operations is the denial of existential value, visible, e.g., in the status of illegal immigrant given to many of the slaughterhouse workers in the United States, which means they are working illegally and without protection (Freshour 2019). These points highlight how the current meat system comes as a package. Thus, if one starts to erode even one the cornerstones of the processes required for the cheapening of meat, the system is not able to function as well as it did before. In fact, this system exists in a continual crisis as suggested by the constant need for higher doses of antibiotics, subsidies from governments, and labor-migrant policies that serve to offer a precarious (and thus more exploitable) workforce for the industry. Extractivisms are a crisis. They not only cause the global crises, but they are the global crises, through their continued day-to-day existence, which is given more value and space, and the power to devour places and lives.

Time is of the essence in the ongoing drive to make meat production global through quickening, mechanizing, and intensification. This process of extending and deepening the global industrial livestock system has also created its own vocabularies and metrics of value, whereby the faster one is able to get the meat (that is, the less time the animal lives) the more profitable the operations. One of the key metrics this meat extractivism carries is the calculation of killings done per minute. For example, Cargill's new poultry factory in China's Anhui Province "employs more than four thousand people and processes 225 birds per minute (bpm), which amounts to more than 65 million chickens per year" (Freshour 2019, 123, drawing on He 2013). The current pace of global capitalism and the inherent, daily damage done to the planet is done within a particular rhythm of time. That is a time, which is lived at a specific pace. Those human beings who subjected to a logic dominated by the killings done per minute, see their quality of life and time drastically deteriorating. Freshour (2019, 136) analyzes how:

> Not only are workers disciplined by the pace of work, but even after their shift ends, workers' "free time" is hardly free, spent recuperating for the next day, buying aspirin and gels at the dollar store. Their very lives are sped up, with a majority of workers experiencing "premature disability," in which they must piece together a living from a monthly disability check.

Mezzadra and Neilson (2019) emphasize that these practices make use of the differentiation of some people as belonging to other "races" or minorities, to make profits based on such overall socio-ethnic cleavages. This is especially clear when observing the colonial and capitalist trajectory of expanding slavery-based plantations, which continues to this day in different forms within the plantation-logic (Murphy and Schroering 2020). Slavery is a form of stripping and stealing others of their time, by ordering what they must do, and in what rhythm.

Of key importance in thinking about time and existences is the rhythm, or the living of time, in which one is posited when living within extractivist or nonextractivist circles. As Gan et al. (2017, 5) describe, "the massive increase in carbon dioxide, methane, and nitrate emissions into the atmosphere from industrialized agriculture, mineral extraction, petroleum-driven production, and globalized shipping/transportation networks has outpaced all other rhythms of life." These extractivist violences will cause a massive number of deaths that will continue into the unforeseeable future, as they have already changed the rhythm of birth and death, as an ever-larger number of animals are born and die in meat factories every day. Some are already living a radically shorter life than what was typical for their kin just a few decades ago. In addition, global extractivisms operate by extracting and redistributing time. The above example shows how the time of so-called production animals is dramatically and violently redistributed. From a human perspective, this redistribution is visible in the creation of leisure classes of people who can afford to live as idle or speculative rentiers. These people exist in the financial and real estate markets, and wield incredible influence over the lives of people whose whole waking time is used for monotonous work to sustain themselves and their families. This system also produces people whose time does not matter (Li 2010), who the process sees as nobodies, or worse, as resistance that must be suppressed or killed.

The plantation-model, with its redistribution of existences, has many impacts and influences power relations across the globe, locking-in numerous changes. The continuing cheap price of feed has made it much harder to steer away from increasing industrialized meat production, given the cheapness of this option in comparison to alternative options. The transformation of flex crops, where, e.g., soybeans and corn are squeezed for their oil, to make biofuels and cooking oils, and many other products, has transformed the markets so that the feed is often not the only product anymore, or even the main product line (Oliveira and Schneider 2016). This facilitates the current boom of installing corn ethanol facilities within monoculture plantations, which deepens the agroextractivist expansion of these regions, as I saw first-hand in late 2019, in the Brazilian Cerrado and the Amazon. Encountering these facilities was shocking as even Brazilian researchers working on soybeans were not yet aware of their existence. This also creates pressures around the world, as profit margins are contracting due to the rising costs of pesticide, fertilizer, machinery, and seed. The agroextractivist model creates a need for higher inputs as the soil vitality depletes and pests increase. For now, the installation of corn ethanol provides the extra profits that this system needs to be able to expand further into the Amazon and other forests. I heard this from farmers and read this in the producers' magazines that were available in the lobbies of the hotels along the BR163 highway between Cuiabá and Santarém. The producers explained that they did not gain profits by planting corn, but that they used corn only as a cover crop. Now that they are able to make ethanol out of corn, in these places far from sources of fossil fuel, which can be used in their machineries and cars, they gain the necessary profit margins to expand the soybean-corn complex. They can also use this transformation to market their agro-extractivism as some sort of climate smart agriculture, hiding behind the rhetoric of a green or bioeconomic transformation. However, these are empty and misleading marketing tactics, as the overall function of the agroextractivism is still to deforest and turn the regions into barren and toxic areas, mostly to produce feed for highly polluting meat processing operations.

These sites of extraction are essential points for maintaining and expanding the global capitalist system. As Moore (2015) and Patel and Moore (2017) argue, these commodities are not cheap naturally, but that they are actively cheapened. This cheapening of commodities should not be seen as benign events of capital accumulation, rather they are, at their very core, repeated events of killing and redistributing existences. A slice of the web of life is taken, its value as life is denied or overlooked, and then it is killed. The future kin of those killed are not given the possibility to be born, live, and evolve in the web of relations that the killed human or other-than-human had before being killed. Instead, another set of life-forms are installed in that place and other similar places along the so-called commodity chain. These transformations are essential for capitalism to be able to operate in the web of life, and to gain the required appropriation of surplus value for all kinds of accumulation operations (see Moore 2015).

Thus, it is essential to observe the source and not only the consumer or productive patterns at the end-markets. The real-world is a place with limits, not the place as it is imagined by economists, where one could extract forever. I have previously argued that the resistance to global extractivisms is a key tool in reversing global problems (Kröger 2020a). As these resistance efforts, one by one, discontinue and block destructive investment projects, such as the expansion of open-pit mining over living forests. All global problems are in fact always regionally-situated and place-based, and need to be solved in those places. Though capital tends to flee and find other places to target for extraction, this is not an automatic or assured process, whereby the capital in question would always succeed.

Places differ and the world is not homogenous. This means that politics of extraction always have place-specific dynamics.[1] In the real capitalist economy, there are no free markets, where production could move wherever without costs and consequences. There is also resistance to the global extractivist moves that varies radically. Such politics are drawing more and more on the understanding that what is now at stake are the lives of all beings on the planet. This message is being taken and distributed by an ever wider group of actors, including elites that support the ecocide criminalization campaign, and have increased demands for corporations to respect human rights, and to be punished for violations. The United Nations' Committee on Economic, Social and Cultural Rights has issued decisions that demand states must investigate the human rights violations of their corporations abroad. Those whose rights have been violated, should also "be able to access effective remedies" (Finnish Ministry of Foreign Affairs 2021). While these seem to be just tiny steps toward a greater recognition of the rights of all humans, it is important to note that these decisions are part of a centuries-old process where capital has been resisted. These struggles fundamentally revolve around expanding rights to ever-larger groups of actors. These politics have been enabled through ontological openings, where the understanding is that actors like women or non-white populations also have enough merit to have rights. This increases the understanding, recognition, and possibly also respect of who actually gets to live a life with agency, and who and what can still be subject to being commodified and turned into a nonliving object serving accumulations. Well into the nineteenth century, enslaving people due to their origins and ethnicity was considered a legal and Christian activity in Brazil, the South of the United States, and many other places. There are steps being taken which seem to lead from the shackles of white Western colonialism, whose violences are not limited to the slave trade from Africa, or to humans, but are nevertheless dramatic in their impacts in the whole web of life and existences.

This is not only a politics that takes place in the sphere of worker struggles against capital, or consumer choices. It is a deeply rooted politics based on defending life, and the possibilities to retain and continue to have life in its varied forms. These struggles often arise in the places where the endless and always increasing accumulation of resources transforms the landscape—relegated to the logic of simply a collateral damage—into a barren, void, toxic place, which is discarded once extracted. These struggles and conflicts come in many forms because there is such a multiplicity of diverse actors involved, including humans and other-than-humans. This can be seen especially clearly when extractivisms meet Indigenous populations.

There are dangers in conducting an analysis of violences through a Western modernist lens, because this can signify being a part of an ontological colonial project of imposing one's Western concepts. For example, even a concept like dispossession suggests that all people would consider that they could own or possess a piece of land (see Nichols 2020). There are some Indigenous people who experience that they are not merely a human, but sometimes they are also a were-jaguar (Kohn 2013), or Afro-Brazilian Quilombos who see the spirit-human interface in very distinct ways in comparison to Christian views. There are also many other examples that suggest there is a whole world, a world of worlds, beyond the modern lexicon focusing just on humans (de la Cadena and Blaser 2018).

The dynamics of violences and their relations to existences have also gained attention from the studies on necropolitics and necroeconomy, wherein differing meanings and uses have been given to these concepts (e.g., Banerjee 2008; Mbembé 2019). However, the angle of these studies is mostly different from what I have proposed in this book, based on the South American Political Ontology, extractivisms, and extinctions literatures. Future studies should pursue analysis that identifies the complementarities between these approaches. One would be the broadening of what exists and should be given value beyond modern multiculturalism, based on Amerindian conceptions of what exists and how. This discussion is just starting, and has recently gained some entrances to national and international legal frameworks and policy-recommendations, this is visible in the rights given to the Mother Earth in some constitutions, or the IPBES (2019a) report, which draws on Indigenous knowledges. IPBES intends in 2021 to include even more input from Indigenous groups on how it should catalogue the wide spectrum of life and the changes of life on the planet. This broadening of the understanding of what exists, and whose lives should be recognized, respected, cared for, and approached reciprocally instead of extractively, should be seen as a process of giving more value to *all* lives, not as a battle for rights between beings, which would worsen the rights or value of, e.g., human beings or a particular human group (as one angry commentator seemed to have misunderstood when I presented these findings in Lima at the Institute of Peruvian Studies in

2017, [RedGe Peru, 2017]). Instead of primarily examining or merely emphasizing the deaths caused and the overarching role of death in capitalist processes, the existing analyses of necroeconomy and necropolitics, could also be accompanied by more detailed analyses of the resistances to these processes. Around the world there are many existing and emerging examples of resistance, and all show how transformations to extractivisms can be generated.

The above notes on the centrality of devaluing certain life-forms and human existences is telling of the key importance of symbolic violence (see Bourdieu 1991) in allowing extractivist expansions, and the accumulation of their gains by a very limited group of humans. These practices within the symbolic space are essential, as they create symbolic power, and they are interlinked with the transformation of the physical and social spaces (Kröger 2016a, 2020a). It is through action within all of these spaces, and their capital distributions, that capital is accumulated, through processes of devaluing life; thus, creating "nobodies," in the billions within humanity, and in the trillions on the animal farms, and in even greater numbers in the spheres that are often left unaccounted for in the web of life. It is essential to link these processes of capital accumulation to the bodily, physical, and territorial changes that occur in particular places, which are much more than abstract spaces of existence to the existences in these lived environments. These existences cannot be exchanged or compensated. It is essential to link analyses to such spaces and particular places and their beings, and avoid the abstract analyses that are typical to some fields and disciplines, e.g., economics.

## Which processes, logics, and actors drive extractivisms?

Who are responsible for these violences in the web of life? Consumers are currently given a lot of attention via the argument that their choices are responsible for and could change what is produced, and how sustainably those items are produced. However, this belief is problematic and shows a fundamental lack of understanding of production systems and the politics related to extractivisms. Individual consumers do not have a full range of choices in all locations, and the market is definitely not defined by some invisible hand that adjusts everything according to some rationale. Rather, the choices consumers get are defined by the power of the regionally dominant political economic actors (such as corporations, industry, and lobby groups), which can define how particular regions are used, and what is or is not produced or available in them. Production systems around the world get bombarded by soybeans and corn—wherever they can be freely and cheaply transported to—because they are produced as cheaply as possible in massive quantities in places like monoculture plantations in Brazil.

There is a tendency to think that due to the length and complexity of global logistical chains, those further up the value chain could or should not be charged for any wrongdoings further down the chain. Even when there is a demonstrable top-down pressure to commit all sorts of cheapening acts. Tsing (2018) opens up these dynamics, explaining how such logistical maneuvers extract value, lives, and worsen the quality of life. For example, these dynamics make the lives of women working in the textile industry extremely precarious and their quality of life miserable in many parts of the world. These processes use up the workers in much the same way agroextractivist processes use up the soil. Moore (2015) refers to the distinct accumulation logics of appropriation and exploitation, wherein appropriation is based on plunder and not paying anything, while the exploitation refers to paying at least something. Typically, the appropriation refers to what is considered to be part of "nature," while the exploitation is refers to those who can earn a wage and thus, they can be part of society. There is often much more appropriation of these cheap "surplus" populations happening in the value-adding parts of the chain than exploitation, which would give at least a living wage.

The agroextractivist operations in northern Mato Grosso are a visible demonstration of a white settler colonial project and its myriad results. The colonialization started in the 1970s with the dictatorial state giving away the land use rights to white settlers from the South of Brazil. At first this extinguished the lives that were already existing in the region, and later created a whole new array of what is given the right to exist in the region. This extractivism has continually operated through a deforesting and genocidal logic. This includes ethnocide and ecocide, dismantling or overlooking the practices of the region and the prior knowledges of what existed in the area before the extraction. The dramatic existential redistributions caused by this process are what these white settler colonialists most essentially "produce"—not the soybeans. However, they are constantly trying to legitimize the soybean as the only thing in the region that should be considered as *production*, which allows them to legitimize themselves as the *producers*, while others in the region are not because they are not involved in the soybean trade. Similar processes explain why many parts of the United States, Canada, Australia, and South Africa have been transformed to large extent into sources of extractivist operations, with huge mines, toxic agroextractivist operations, meat-producing enclaves, and other emblems that illustrate the kind of limited spectrum of existences that the power driving these colonialisms wants to materialize on the ground.

The creation of ethnic and racial cleavages and inferiorities and superiorities, imposed especially by Europeans/whites, is a key logic that is extended, and underlies the capital accumulation according to Murphy and Schroering (2020). Large parts of the Amazon, Cerrado, and Atlantic forests of Brazil have been colonized by European-descendant Brazilians, via the genocides of Indigenous populations and violences against Afro-Brazilian communities and other traditional populations. The centrality of racial categorizations alongside and in the speeches of those who continue to expand the plantations support these claims. Since I began doing interviews in 2004, I have heard many pejorative and shocking references made by white representatives of the Brazilian paper and pulp industry, and the soybean farmers, against the Indigenous and Afro-Brazilian populations, especially those that resisted their plantation expansions. For example, one director of a pulp industry lobby organization said to me during our 2006 interview in a fancy São Paulo office, "can you believe that there are now even whites supporting the struggles of the blacks in Espirito Santo," against the expansion of eucalyptus plantations by the Aracruz corporation (which had been extended into the Afro-Brazilian Quilombo communities' forests). These discourses reflect the devaluation of most human lives on the planet by extractivists, based on ethnic and other categorizations. The devaluation of existences is the overall logic behind these speeches and their congruent extractivist moves, extractivist logics, and practices seeking to extract as much as possible, especially from those who have been designated as not worthy of having as much as others.

With the complex power-relations and asymmetries behind global extractivisms, I argue that the Anthropocene, a popular term, which aims to describe the current era of the world is not actually an accurate description, as a much more precise analysis is needed to lay the responsibility where it belongs. The concept of Anthropocene assumes that some sort of monolithic Anthropos exists; however, this assumption flattens the responsibility of all people and nations within the global crisis (e.g., oil corporation directors are just as culpable as Indigenous people) (Moore 2016). This is not to say that there are not some others than the European-descendant settlers and elites who would not also be responsible in some cases—yet, these violences mostly also take place in a Western-dominated world (see Escobar 2020, 2021; Kothari et al. 2019). For example, the responsibility of an ex-rubber tapper from the Amazon, who is pressured by surrounding cattle capitalists to cede lands for deforestation, often by coercion, differs from the responsibility of the rancher. The illegal renting of lands by forest-dwellers for deforesting activities are more of an enabling factor than the responsibility held by the cattle capitalists pushing these moves (Kröger 2020d). While the prior agency eases and allows the extractivist expansion, to certain extent, the latter agency is a necessary causal factor for the extractivism to even exist to be able to push and drive its way into new areas. These dynamics of driving and enabling factors behind extractivist processes need to be studied in much more detail to be fully understood. This understanding will be helpful in clarifying the terms of how the responsibility is shed, in this moment of rising accounts based on neo-Malthusian views, wherein the Western media portrays poor peasants or Africans as the key culprits of deforestation and destruction. It is ironic that often the people responsible for the violences blame the victims for the ills created; a prime example of this is Bolsonaro's government in Brazil.

The disrespect of life that Bolsonaro has demonstrated, especially during the COVID-19 pandemic, has led to a growing number of people calling his attitudes genocidal. This is especially true when considering Indigenous peoples, whose lives and rights have under Bolsonaro seen a similar kind of "avalanche of attacks" that were released on them in the 1964–1984 dictatorship in Brazil (dos Santos 2020, 427). Many analysts are surprised by the total disrespect and sudden eradication of the progresses in terms of rights that the 1988 Constitution, international agreements, and the socio-environmental movement had created in Brazil since the 1980s. The debates around these themes often revolve around who has the right to exist, and how. The Bolsonaro regime sees itself as a messiah, brought to save the Indigenous people from their false consciousness imposed by NGOs and foreigners who supposedly want to prevent them and Brazil from "developing."

Several new studies of Brazil, utilizing the framework of extractivism, argue that Bolsonaro pursues an agenda where only extractivisms are allowed. This means that peasant, smallholder, landless movement, Quilombo, Indigenous, and other family farming and food producing models are not supported in any way, but are instead attacked, and agricultural support is given solely to agroextractivists (Soyer and Barbosa 2020). This support given to extractivism has also been applied in the mining sectors, which the Bolsonaro regime has given the freedom to expand destructive projects on Indigenous lands. The regime has made these extractivist pushes through "connivance with crimes, incentive to illegal practices, undemocratic initiatives, promotion of fake news, intimidation of opposing groups, coercion of State agents, and threats to minority rights" (Wanderley, Gonçalves, and Milanez 2020, 557). These policies are a continuation of the long line of violences, which mark the process of Brazilian territorial formation since the fifteenth century. In these processes, Indigenous people who have been living in their home areas for thousands of years were framed as nobodies, with this process of "nobodization" still continuing, as revealed by the Bolsonaro-supporters' hate speech (Porto-Gonçalves and da Rocha Leão 2020, 721). The mechanisms of routine "nobodization" is also extended to the Afro-Brazilians living in poor neighborhoods, who see that the police treat people living in favelas like the slaves on slave ships (Porto-Gonçalves and da Rocha Leão 2020).

These dynamics are part of a larger extractivist logic that is fundamentally based on the assumptions about who has value and rights, and who does not. Therefore, extractivism is also about existential politics. These politics are at the core of capitalist and other modernist value-making economic actions. This might explain at a deeper level why periodically when the capitalist world-ecology has entered into crises of accumulation, e.g., when sites of extraction have been limited for whatever reason, there has been a surge of support from corporate elites for national-populist political movements. This has often deepened hate and divisions between people of the world, while it upholds the rights of certain privileged human groups at the cost of almost all other forms of life. These sorts of polarizing dynamics are at play in states, such as Brazil and the United States, and might even benefit several large corporations, which publicly remain silent about their stance and actions during the turbulent political times. There is still much to do to merge the existing political economic analyses with the kind of existential thinking proposed in this book.

## Toward a more chaotic world-system and world-ecology?

As the current world-system is strongly characterized by and built on the existential annihilations and redistributions of multiple extractivisms, there is a need to examine the contemporary situation and the future of that system. Extractivisms have already ushered in a chaotic and less balanced or predictable world-system. Therefore, it is useful to ask the questions about whether extractivisms are likely to expand in the coming decades, and with what impacts? World-system analysts and other scholars, e.g., in international relations and anthropology, have discussed the future and the role of capitalism, and I will next link these discussions to the extractivism scholarship, to make some prognoses on what the future could look like.

There are many important aspects of this world-systemic take on extractivisms, which can be uncovered through an exploration of the following questions. How are the recent extractivist expansions and violences in South America and elsewhere related to the overall world-systemic and world-ecological transformations, such as the much-envisaged end of capitalism, or the arrival of a more chaotic world-system era? What is the role of the international system, where nation-states compete with each other for supremacy, and states prioritize national interests and security? How should global extractivisms and existential redistributions be seen in light of these global dynamics, and what can the lessons of this book contribute to those broader debates?

It is important to first link the present to the past, to understand the current international system and its character, key actors, and dynamics. The past 5,000 years have seen the rise of capital and empires, seeking to dominate others (Frank and Gills 1993), which has led to major deforestation and other types of environmental havoc, as forests have been decimated for wood and other materials essential for empire-building (Perlin 2005). This process was intensified during the fifteenth century with the wars of European nation-states. Jumping to the contemporary era, the past two decades have seen the rise of China as a new global power, as well as the other BRICS and few other nations as well, which is the most important reason explaining the concomitant rise of extractivisms, commodity prices, and destruction of existences. However, the current inter-state system, with its inbuilt battles and logic of supremacy and domination over others—a competition of nations, as envisaged by world leaders—cannot continue much longer in the same manner, as the planet cannot sustain such a system. The material bases of accumulation of capital and power to some states and their linked corporations are now reaching such a limit, such that the key goals of striving for security and power are undermined by such attempts. Klare (2019) explains in *All Hell Breaking Loose* how the Pentagon is already getting ready for the situation when climate and other crises will become uncontrollable, and other armed forces are also more concerned about the ecological crises and are preparing for it more proactively than most politicians.

It seems that the world may become ever-more chaotic, due to the converging global crises of environmental collapses, emergencies, and extinctions of species, life forms, habitats, and macro-ecosystems, which are the pillars on which life as we know it on this planet has relied on for the past millennia. Pandemics, such as COVID-19, and ecologic crises, are bound to become much more regular occurrences if nothing is done to reduce the global threat of antibiotic-resistance and the feed-meat complex, which is risking global food supplies and extracting life. Pandemics seem to be closely related to increasing deforestation and extinctions (Tollefson 2020), and deforesting activities are also one of the root causes of increasing chaos in international relations. The different paths taken by countries—such as Jair Bolsonaro's Brazil—suggest that some regions of the world will be (and already are) much more chaotic and unlivable than others.

The inter-state system, with its competition for power and the resulting wars, has been a key cause (or even the main cause) for explaining why forests have been so wantonly destroyed for thousands of years, and especially during the past 550 years. Histories of forests and logging tell a clear picture of how huge natural forest areas were destroyed primarily through the process of inter-state competition and wars of the emerging European colonial powers during the past 550 years (Moore 2015; Perlin 2005). The demand for masts for imperial ships, tar, and blanks for building sailing vessels ate entire forests in the Eastern United States (Perlin 2005). The monoculture plantations required cutting down firewood, which was brought quickly from outside of the colonial islands to the plantation operations, to enrich the war-making modern states. In sum, the violence and quest for power by European elites was in essence a war on forests. This was in no way a rational or enlightened process. Countless fleets of warships, things made out of wood, and other stripped parts of the living nature, were sunk, wasted, burned, pillaged, ravaged, forgotten, and used thoughtlessly. This state of affairs still continues, as seen in the enormous bootprints of the modern military machineries, as Belcher et al. (2019) call the weight of militaries in the global geopolitics of ecology. Future analyses of geopolitical ecology also need to consider the way armed forces of different types are related to the four key questions, to the expansion or resistance of extractivisms, and the existences of beings. Their role in today's Brazil is certainly key, as the Bolsonaro regime is in essence a military government, which uses its own logics to deepen extractivisms and disregard life (Penido and da Gama Janot 2021). Therefore, if the ultimate causes of extractivisms are sought after, they must be searched for in the international system and its dynamics, laws, and key actors, which are not the same as governments or states, but include more specific actor-categories, such as the armed forces.

Future research should also pay attention to how extractivisms through their existentially redistributive dimensions influence state creation processes within the international system, and what are the bases of modern nation-state creations in terms of their costs to existing lives and future possibilities of living. For example, there are some who contend that Greenland could mine its way to independence, via mega-mining projects, including many Indigenous Greenlanders who would like to create a modern nation-state based on mining revenues (Kuokkanen 2017). However, such understandings are based on an outdated understanding of the current global situation and the character of extractivist expansions. Given the extractivist and unsustainable character of this kind of path, it would not be feasible, as once the mega-mining projects would have theoretically created the needed flows of money to redeem what was lost from the Danish aid, Greenland itself would be devastated. At least 24 new large mines would need to be opened, this providing only some quick money, but no real solution (Rosing et al. 2014). The process would also not be politically feasible due to resistance (EurActiv 2021). Analyses of the nation-state-existences interface should also keep in mind the note that extractivisms not only destroy, but also create possibilities for something new to arise. However, these new things may not be good at all, and might start to act in their own rights as political tools. An example of this is the case of genetically manipulated crops that have been shown to cause biological contamination to nearby fields and other natural environments (Cummings 2008). These negative impacts can also be seen with other extractivist technologies and infrastructures, which have been expensive to create, with their sunk costs imposing needs and path dependencies to continue using them.

Most social scientific and political analysis is still done as if the ecological crises and forthcoming climatic catastrophes do not exist. Thus, they offer a false view of the world, with erroneous prognoses, and an analysis of the past that does not help enough in developing an understanding of what should be done now, or how things will be in the future. This is the case with most international relations scholarship, where the presence of climate crisis discussions is not yet being taken seriously, and is just starting to be adopted in research. Consolidating nation-states and governments worried about their geopolitical status or pressured within the international system to allow for imperial or multinational capital expansions over their territories have been key actors in expanding extractivisms with major existential impacts, including the kinds of extinctions of Indigenous populations and deforestation that are discussed to make the case of the partial "internal colonialism" of the Amazon highlighted herein. This is done within the capitalist world-system, whose key dynamic is competing and partially isolated, cores and centers of accumulation of capital linked to particular states, although the power of financial markets to dictate the patterns of extraction has recently increased extremely (Woodley 2015). For van Apeldoorn, de Graaff, and Overbeek (2012), the massive bailouts that financial corporations received after the 2008 financial crisis (that they themselves caused) combined with their practical impunity, suggests that currently financial capital is the real sovereign, and not the states that rescue it and obey its commands. This is reinforced by a marked lack of change in the system since the 2008 crisis. There is a need to look more deeply into the role of financing of extractivist operations, and the impacts this has for existences.

What happens when more chaos takes place? Does this signify a less "dynamic" or systematic looting of the earth, for the sake of war-making? Might there be a greater possibility for pockets of peace to emerge, where nonextractivist relations would start to blossom, as sites of care and rebirth, rising from the ashes of "sacrifice zones"?

No process is eternal or can truly manage to get a complete grip and control over natural processes, even those processes that displace forests and are based on thousands or millions of hectares of monocultures. The expansion of mega-plantations that started in the nineteenth century and restarted in earnest in many parts of the world since the 1980s will most likely still continue "for quite some time" complete with their radical transformation of landscapes and replacement of existing human and other-than-human lived environments (Kenney-Lazar and Ishikawa 2019, 63). Tsing (2018) considers scalability to be a key mechanism to explain how and why modern capitalist thinking expands to new frontiers. She also emphasizes that despite this constant expansion of logic and new technologies that augment the scale, via a scalability imperative, there is always life that remains, and new possibilities in the pockets that could not be scaled, or in the ruins of the areas where resource frontiers have passed. This gives more hope to the future of post-extractivist worlds.

Wallerstein et al.'s *Does Capitalism Have a Future?* (2013) is one of the studies that predicts that the capitalist system will break down in the coming two or three decades. Capitalists will find it harder or impossible to invest in the same way as before, as they are now pressured by rising socio-ecological costs. The era of the last 500 years where a system was in place for the elite in the cores to accumulate profits relatively securely is about to reach its systemic limitations. This capitalism is just one historic system. Both Collins (2013) and Wallerstein (2013) argue that the decades around 2040 will be a time of full-scale capitalist crisis, especially due to severe ecological damages.

Wallerstein (2011, 36) foresees "sharp rises in the costs of all the basic inputs both to production and daily life—energy, food, water, breathable air," for which reason moments and pockets of respite from the overall chaotic setting are likely to be short-lived.

The current capitalist world-system has been, according to Wallerstein (2011, 35) in a structural crisis since the 1970s. This is visible in the "rapid and constant fluctuations" in "the world-economy, the interstate system, and cultural-ideological currents, but also the availability of life resources, climatic conditions, and pandemics." This setting is characterizable as chaos, which is deeply rooted in the destruction of life by extractivisms. In this setting, Wallerstein argues that the most important short-term task is to minimize pain. This would entail actions, such as giving support for just transitions or farming land to workers unemployed as extractivist operations are discontinued. As longer-term tasks, Wallerstein (2011, 37) lists replacing the search for economic growth with "maximum decommodification," e.g., via Buen Vivir and other Indigenous approaches. These approaches fundamentally transform the current forms of agriculture and industry, as well as education, health systems, and the commodification(s) of the body, air, and water. Wallerstein also calls for local and regional sovereignty for food and living compounds. In relation to existences, Moore (2016, 11) goes deeper in this analysis, arguing that the most promise is found in the kind of ontological politics and revaluations of life that this book has discussed, "We see as never before the lowering of an ontological imagination beyond Cartesian dualism, one that carries forth the possibility of alternative valuations of food, climate, nature, and everything else." Wallerstein (2011) is more wary of the possibilities, emphasizing that such activities may be able to help establish a better world-system, but there are also great dangers that the forthcoming system will be worse than the current one. The future is still open, and much will depend on political actions, and possible irreversible ecological collapses, deep pandemics, or nuclear wars.

Much of the current prognoses of geopolitics and the rise of new powers are premised on an understanding where the current and forthcoming ecological catastrophes are not taken into account.[2] This is evident by looking at what is happening in India due to Prime Minister Modi's push to increase coal-production, Bolsonaro's deforesting, and China's policies that are increasing extractivisms globally and also coal- and other polluting production nationally. This is also visible in the continued and long-established violences of the Western powers. Mann (2013) emphasizes that the ecological catastrophes, which will hit the Global South especially hard, including the rising global powers from these areas, which will make it unlikely that they will become the next global hegemons. Mann also sees that capitalism can overcome most of its barriers, and continue, as he thinks there are only a few things capable of putting an end to it, like nuclear war or a deep planetary collapse. Moore (2015), however, contrasts such views of capitalism, arguing that they overlook that capitalism is a capitalism-in-nature, with nature included in it, and it is not possible for it to continue without cheap natures, whose production are quickly becoming much more difficult, due to capitalism's internal contradictions. Livingston (2019) offers a similar account of the Global South countries which seek to emulate capitalist growth patterns, and explains how this is a form of self-devouring growth.

There are several other new studies on the current capitalist system that liken the impacts of capitalism and capital to the aforementioned necropolitics and extinctions. For example, McBrien (2016) argues that capital accumulation is premised on causing extinctions, and thus it is apt to call this necrotic process accumulation by extinction. If one looks at the extinctions caused in the past decades and centuries, one finds ample empirical evidence to support such an overall claim. When going into the details, as in this book, one sees how specific agroextractivisms operate via causing extinctions. Thus, McBrien (2016) calls the current era not as the Anthropocene or Capitalocene, but the Necrocene. The world-ecological theorizations that draw on this understanding, emphasize that unless barriers are put to capital accumulation, in the form of mobilizations and state regulation, "capitalists are driven to exploit and appropriate labor and nature to the maximum" (Walker and Moore 2019, 63). Yet, as capitalism exists as capitalism-in-nature and relies on new frontiers to accumulate, it is vulnerable and not very resilient when commodity prices rise. This seems to be happening now, as I discussed through the concept of the commodity paradigm, where most raw material priccs continuc to be much higher than they were before 2005. Moorc (2017b, 177) also sees the rising resistance and climate disruptions as signaling an end to the "Cheap Nature model," whereby the "mechanisms of cheapening labor, food, energy, and raw materials" are being reversed and made impossible due to irreversible, nonlinear metabolic shifts of the planet and of capitalist appropriation itself. Moore argues that this is not because of some imagined external limits to capital, such as end of physical space, but more due to the logic of capitalist accumulation not being able to continue through its basic modes of appropriating unpaid labor to a greater extent than exploiting the paid labor.

Currently, "new streams of unpaid work are materializing slowly, if at all," and furthermore, "the accumulation of waste and toxification is now threatening the unpaid work that is being done" (Moore 2014, 308). Moore sees that the climate crisis makes it impossible to renew an agricultural revolution that would reproduce cheap food. Furthermore, the amount of unpaid work that humans in the United States and other places are now doing is already maximized, and cannot be increased anymore, as showcased by burnout and other mental health issues across the Global North, which implies that no more unpaid work can be delivered for capital accumulation processes. Moore (2014) sees that this means the rise in the price of commodified products, such as labor, food, energy, and raw materials, and as their price increases there will be far fewer possibilities for capital accumulation. Profits are what sustain capitalisms of different types, as well as overall global capitalism, where macroeconomic policies require constant gross domestic product (GDP) growth and yearly dividends from the stock portfolios of pension funds. When these premises start to shatter, it will have major consequences for the so-called modern industrial economies. Mitchell (2011) implies that these industrial economies are mostly possible due to cheap energy in the form of fossil fuels. Western liberal democracies might be standing on quicksand, which they will sink into once energy and other costs need to be addressed, assuming of course one wants to avoid climatic calamities.

This explains in more detail how capitalism is becoming weaker, as the things that unpaid nature does for capitalism are changing and offer less in return in the future. Moore (2017b, 178) does not thus consider that capitalism would be "all powerful," but instead sees that it is "self-defeating," as the "places where food, energy, raw materials and workers can be drawn for free or low cost"—capitalism being dependent on such frontiers—are not boundless, and these have caused such destruction that the impacts are also negative for the capitalists themselves. This challenges the viewpoint of scholars, such as Mann (2013), on what capitalism fundamentally is and how it would be able to continue despite the growing and irreversible extinctions, which will make certain activities like farming much more expensive, or even impossible, and will increase the demand to curb the agribusiness model. The agroextractivist expansion relies on rising greenhouse gas emissions, soil depletion, reliance on petrochemicals, and the use of agrotoxics. Thus, it consumes the places that lie in its path and it needs new frontiers to consume via deforestation. The Amazon is already at a tipping point and seems to be causing more greenhouse gas emissions than it is absorbing, as so much of the forest has been burned and turned into pastures and plantations that emit carbon, methane, and other gases (Covey et al. 2021). On top of that, global emissions are making it harder to stop these processes of deforesting the Amazon. This means that sooner, rather than later, the agribusiness plantations south of the Amazon may face a similar kind of ecological collapse as the prairies in the United States, which were degraded, with increasing droughts and other problems linked to the savannization. In such irreversible processes, fire often takes the command from humans. In contemporary Brazil, fires are lit by (some) humans.

In my view, there are many ways in which such socio-ecological crises could affect politics, as the rise of Bolsonaro, Trump, Modi, and many other leaders that are hostile toward life in the midst of worsening planetary crises suggests. In 2019, in support of Bolsonaro and to show that they can do what they want, land grabbers and speculators in the Amazon started an event called a Day of Fire, igniting fires in several large, protected areas in the Brazilian Amazon, especially near the frontier town of Novo Progresso and elsewhere along the BR163 in the Southwest of Pará. While most of the responsible parties were identified, many were not punished or fined (Barbosa 2020). Instead, Bolsonaro blamed the actor Leonardo DiCaprio for supposedly giving cash to light the Amazon fires (BBC News 2019). Bolsonaro had the backing of military personnel and significant segments of the Brazilian population. It is important to note how such, irrational and delusional actions and speeches arise at the moment when the Amazon is identified as being at a tipping point, where no more deforestation can occur. These are examples of what the current and deepening chaotic period looks like. There are also many other quite incredible stories—importantly, all told with an air of supremacy, contempt, and hate toward those who do not believe them—which have gained root among a surprisingly large and powerful group of people in Brazil and elsewhere. For example, eleven million Brazilians believe that the world is flat rather than round, and they call contrary views conspiracies (Trouillaud 2020). As a sufficient amount of powerful people support or believe such claims, it is no wonder that extractivisms are expanded in and through the midst of chaos. The rise of such absurdities reflects the view of Danowski and Viveiros de Castro (2017) according to which violences are expanding ever-faster, possibly leading to an era of barbarisms, with the unfolding crisis being unforeseen, unimaginable, and thus uncertain and unpredictable.

In contrast to such prognoses of uncertainty and barbarity, there are also more hopeful accounts. For example, Patomäki (2017, 115) sees that there is "a tendential rational direction to world history—grounded in institutionally enabled and facilitated existential security and trust—toward global Keynesianism, global social justice and global democracy." Patomäki suggests that what is needed in this period of post-capitalist transition is holoreflexivity, which is a holistic, global, and planetary reflection encompassing all that lives. Drawing on Camilleri and Falk (2009, 537), who explain how holoreflexivity "is global in that it encompasses all social groupings, communities, cultures and civilisations, and planetary in that it comprises the totality of relationships between the human species and the rest of the biosphere," Patomäki (2017) opens up several budding tendencies toward such a direction. Thus, there is hope, but this relies on democratizing the global spheres to avoid powerful actors from dictating the rules and moral conceptions (Patomäki 2017, 121). Much depends on politics and agency, and very little is decided.

To get a better idea of the many resistances around the world, which go mostly unnoted by the Western or other media, more study of and exposure to lives around the world is needed. Detailed and systematic political analysis should be conducted to understand the causalities that are emerging in this setting, to see the complexities involved in the interface of rising mobilizations, or the lack thereof, and the outcomes of extractivist investment projects, including a vast array of different explanatory factors, such as contingencies (Kröger 2021). Given the overall depth of the current crises, and unwillingness by the elites for resolution, it is possible that other-than-human nature will come to play a much bigger and visible role, e.g., in the form of ever-worse pandemics. As viruses are not being taken seriously or curbed, they will become more central and uncontrollable players in the global arena. Ironically, this will be the case especially where the existences of extra-human actors are denied, in line with an overall deep anthropocentrism and mockery of life, as in Bolsonaro's Brazil, as already visible in the current chaos and collapse of the society, and several ecological systems.

However, the chaos bred in these sites will not remain there, due to the increasing interconnection in the world, as the spread of COVID-19 and its variants have shown. Yet, there are possibilities to turn the tide and make changes to avert future catastrophes if there is political will. This was shown in 2004–2011, which was a period of rapid slowdown of the deforestation in the Amazon. The efforts by many nations to curb the expansion of COVID-19 are also hopeful signs that when existences are threatened, the economy can be put in second place. The key now is to make decision-makers understand that action needs to be taken pre-emptively and one cannot wait for ecological crises and irreversible tipping points to materialize. There are already many people working toward this goal, in many ways.

## Key questions for integrating analysis of existences to current studies

This book has proposed and shown how to apply four key questions for studying existences:

1. Who or what exists?
2. How they can exist (what is the quality of existence)?
3. In which time and/or how long they exist?
4. Who are the key entities deciding and contesting the rights to exist?

More study is required on these questions, and this book offers a framework and an example of how to analyze existences based on empirical materials collected via field research. These questions can be used as a structuring guideline for articles, books, and theses, to assist in thinking about the world in a new way. These key questions can also guide the way field research is conducted, to be more aware of the wide range of existences when conducting political ecological and other analysis. I have tried to be as broad as possible in terms of what kinds of existences to consider, drawing from Amazon Indigenous and other viewpoints, to go beyond Western and modern valuations and vocabularies. These perspectives offer ontological openings that are essential, in my view, to offer deeper solutions, logics, and practices to solve the current global crises. The four key questions can also be used to explore transformative alternatives to extractivisms, that is, anti-extractivist actions and movements, which are physically challenging and trying to reverse the expansions of extractivism. An example of an anti-extractivist movement is the Brazilian Landless Movement, which tries to implant an agroecological agrarian reform. As Chapter 2 showed, via an exploration of the types and degrees of extractivisms, the key questions can also open up and relativize the role of non extractivist practices. The questions can also be applied to better understand the role that political economic actors and systems have in different sectors, including both hyper extractivist and partially extractivist practices. I recommend such detailed analysis, instead of lumping all resource extraction under the label of extractivism. Besides the suggestion for assessing the degree and type of extractivisms through particular guiding parameters, which I identified based on the existing literature on extractivisms, and via fresh field research, the four key questions offer a wealth of untapped potential for future theoretical innovations and empirical applications. The deeper aspects of the four dimensions, and how they work at the global scale, with multiple and complex impacts on existences throughout sectorial value webs, for all human and all kinds of other-than-human actors, should be explored in more detail.

Scholars should take the perspective of viewing the places that are framed as "resource" or "commodity frontiers" as sites for redefining what can exist from more than just the standpoint of power and capitalist relations, but also in terms of the beings and spectrums and relations of existences. There is a need for such a shift in many vocabularies, as environmental and mainstream economics, or even the emancipatory take on agrarian political economy (often out of convention), do not even speak of, and typically hide through their selection of words to represent the many lives and many existences, at play. This book has used regionally-situated world-ecologies of Brazil and Finland, and brief references to some other places around the world, to illustrate how the analysis of power and agency via agrarian political economy and geopolitical ecology, *together* with the study of existences, can bring forth the many worlds being affected by extractivisms.

Herein, I discuss the current planetary moment of the sixth mass extinction, which is already well on its course (Henderson 2014). This course signifies not only major extinctions, possibly comparable to some of the prior mass extinctions that left alive as little as 5 percent of all species that were in existence but also to the general character of these mass extinctions as an opening of new possibilities for other species to thrive and evolve. Human beings are one result of these past mass extinctions, which created space for new existences. Thus, the concept of existential redistribution captures a fuller sense what happens with, or beside extinctive drives. While humans might also become extinct as a result of this mass extinction (Bradshaw et al. 2021), that process is already in full swing according to some analysts who base their understanding on the dependency of human existence on many other species and relations that are now vanishing, which may open up possibilities for other species and beings to rise from the ashes. Yet, a growing number of studies suggest there are still possibilities to subvert this mass extinction tendency (Berwyn 2021), and these studies offer practical lessons on how to do so. A key stance in this subversion is to avoid "doomism" and be active in reversing the destructive practices (e.g., Boivin and Crowther 2021; Kröger 2020d; Mann 2021). This reversal needs to be based on the understanding that species are actually ways of life, which means that species are not just some abstract, reified, static beings that exist in a vacuum, separated from the practices and life rhythms that make them and their surroundings. Species are part of lived environments and extinction drives of species do not occur only when their numbers fall, or the last being of the species dies, but these extinction drives actually start much earlier, when the ways of life of those species begin to fundamentally change, or are curbed, transformed, and violated. This includes when the most important relations with other species are compromised. These kinds of changes in the quality and temporality of existences are essential to observe, and to use as guidelines to step back from practices that seem to cause such threats to existences, especially via transforming species behavior in fundamental ways.

The understanding of extractivisms as existentially redistributing and extinction-driving processes enables the use of and connects to several contemporary theoretical developments. While there have been studies on different aspects of existences in particular disciplinary discussions, it is rare to see these being merged. This has been one of the impetuses for writing this contribution. This book has united at least three different theoretical strands: (1) world-ecology, wherein capitalism is seen as a frontier in which modern conceptualizations of "nature" are essential for pursuing expansionist policies and the appropriation of unpaid labor, that is, the rest of "nature" that does not need to be paid for its work, or even noticed ("cheap nature") (Moore 2015); (2) the agrarian political economies of commodity frontiers, including their ties to statist and neoliberal processes of accumulation (e.g., Borras et al. 2016; Weis 2013); (3) Political Ontology, wherein what exists and can exist in ecological and environmental conflicts is broadened to include nonmodern entities and beings (e.g., Blaser, 2009; de la Cadena, 2015). By uniting these three strands of theory, the "cheap nature" created by extractivism can be seen as a redistribution of existences, that is the creation of a larger volume of select types of existences that are useful for capital at the cost of destroying or neglecting all other existences.

This book has offered a framework and illustrated how to conduct a political economy of existences. I have argued that the consideration of the existences of both human and other-than-human entanglements should be given more emphasis across the scientific fields, policy-making processes, and in the unique places where these entanglements exist, which cannot be compensated via other places. It is essential that the vocabularies which flatten existences, such as those typical in resource and environmental economics, which treat living beings as numbers that can then be lumped together, need to start to change. Moreover, this change needs to be reflected through practices.

I illustrated through the case of the soybean frontier in Brazil how to apply the four key questions, and what kinds of dimensions should be included within the categories. I invite others to broaden the scale and scope of these analyses, to new areas, scales, and dimensions of existences. I hope the key questions can serve as a tool to add more focus on existences, and to change the way global and regional policy-makers consider life and "natural resources." I have also argued that one should not remain only in the confines of Western modernity, but should seek to include diverse Indigenous viewpoints and understandings of the world as a place of many worlds, whose actor categories and types go well beyond the strict human/non-human dualisms. These suggest a less anthropocentric and more reciprocal, caring worldview, whose cultivation is essential to overcome the burden of past and current extinctions and ongoing extractivisms.

## Notes

1. An example of this is the overall global markets for iron ore, which are a product of these conjoint struggles and dynamics. Iron ore that has a high ore content is not found in many places. Many steel mills operate based on a commodity chain where most of the bulky metal is extracted nearby. Bringing in iron ore from further away would require modernization of the plant, or the lay-off of a large number of workers, which was the case in India's railroad track producing Bhilai Steel Plant in the Chhattisgarh state. As a result of this arithmetic, to supply the steel mill the state-owned plant is implanting violent military operations to try to kill the guerillas and Indigenous Adivasi people resisting their forested hills being turned into open-pit mines (Kröger 2020a).
2. However, see Kröger (2020b and 2020c) for a list of International Relations and related studies that have started to include ecology within geopolitical analysis.

# Epilogue

When I was finishing the process of writing this book in early 2021, Finland had a cold, icy, and snowy winter, reminiscent of the years before the climate emergency, which was surprising after many years of mild winters. The winter weather brought joy and made it possible to practice winter sports in the capital, and around Southern Finland, which had been almost impossible for several years. Was there still hope to revert back to the Holocene's stable climate, which had offered four seasons, and an excellent possibility for human and other lives to thrive? Or was this sign of the new reality of climate disruptions, where abnormal weather extremes can linger in the Northern Hemisphere, due to polar vortex disruptions? In any case, there were many days in March 2021, when sun was shining, and one could walk or ski long distances on top of the thick and firm snow without falling in.

To gain a respite from the intense writing process, I went to ski in a frozen swamp when the snow was firm enough to carry my weight. The path to the swamp is long—across fields, forests, and tree plantations, which surrounded the swamp and make the entrance there very hard and tricky, due to the numerous dikes dug to dry the swampland, and the trees that have been thickly planted. During this time, forests had become more important sites of respite, as friends could not be easily met. Particular, close-by forests became places, and not just any rural space that one passes by. It seemed that I was not the only person experiencing such a transformation in respect and appreciation for forests. This was visible in the heated public criticism of clear-cutting practices in Finland. The place I have been living, Southern Karelia, is a hotspot of Finland's industrial forestry. This province only has 1.7 percent of protected forest, the least amount in all of Finland. Most areas that used to be forest are now tree plantations, degraded, fragmented, spoiled areas with no easy way to walk in them, or even the sensation of being in a forest. Thus, when one arrives to the end of this swamp, where there is an ancient, yet unprotected forest, with fallen trees and moss all around, entering it feels like entering a very unique place. A place that is fragile, and constantly under the threat of being annihilated by one of the mechanical harvesters whose sound could frequently be heard when walking in the area. This standing forest is a gate to the past, a different time, to a sense of what had been here for centuries. Standing looking at it, one could feel a special, different feeling. Before one can enter this forest, one must jump over a quite large dike. In the area, there were frequently bear tracks in the snow, and while it was a delight to see these and other animals' tracks, it also made one a bit wary at times. The last time I was here, a few months earlier, I did not enter the old forest. Standing before it, I had asked silently if I could immerse myself in the forest, but an ominous feeling washed over me and gave me a sense that the answer was no. Thus, I did not enter remembering my past experiences of not listening to such deeply felt cues when asking permission. Perhaps there was a bear sleeping in there or something else that my presence would disturb. On this visit, again I had a wary sensation, when I asked permission to enter. However, because I had made the long journey across the fields and through the thickets, across many dikes, I stayed put at the edge of the forest. I listened intently for any other signs of why I might be having this feeling. After a while, I had a revelation. Perhaps asking permission was not enough, but I needed to actually offer something to whomever or whatever was there. I should not just come there extractively, with the mindset of gaining entrance simply by asking without giving anything in return. So, I reached to my pocket and placed a bit of the snack I had brought with me on the forest floor. I had the feeling that there were important reasons for doing this, mostly beyond explanation, and I did not do this out of any calculation. Immediately after making this offering to the forest, I felt it was okay to enter into this old, mossy haven. This reciprocity was a new experience. This was a learning experience, connected to the forests of the Amazon, that spoke directly to what I had learned from Indigenous people in the Amazon about the need to engage in more reciprocal relations. This means to base the relation on recognition and to show respect to all else that might exist with oneself in particular places. I felt that it was the feeling, practice, and attitude of giving, which was essential, not so much what or how much is given. Rather it is the volition and energy with which one enters a place, by giving and not only taking—a state of mind of not trying to take at all. Practicing such reciprocity, after centuries of extracting, is an important step in the creation of a more balanced life, and a more peaceful being.

# Bibliography

Acosta, Alberto. 2017. "Post-extractivism: From discourse to practice—Reflections for action." In *International Development Policy Volume 9*, edited by Gilles Carbonnier, Humberto Campodónico, and Sergio Tezanos Vázquez, 77–101. Geneva, Switzerland: Brill Nijhoff.
Acosta, Alberto. 2020. "Extractive dependency renewed. Violence against people, territories and visions." In *Indigenous Women & Climate Change*, edited by Rocío Silva-Santisteban, 15–34. Lima, Peru: IWGIA.
Alonso-Fradejas, Alberto. 2020. "The Modern Periphery-Making Machine in the Early Twenty-First Century." *International Review of Social History* 65(3): 507–518. https://doi.org/10.1017/S0020859020000590
Alston, Lee J., Gary D. Libecaps, and Bernando Mueller. 2000. "Land Reform Policies, the Sources of Violent Conflict and the Implications for Deforestation in the Brazilian Amazon." *Journal of Environment and Resource Management* 39(2): 162–88. https://doi.org/10.1006/jeem.1999.1103
Altieri, Miguel A., 2018. *Agroecology: The Science of Sustainable Agriculture*. Boca Raton, FL: CRC Press.
Andrade, Daniela. 2020. "Populism From Above and Below: The Path to Regression in Brazil." *The Journal of Peasant Studies* 47(7): 1470–1496. https://doi.org/10.1080/03066150.2019.1680542
Arboleda, Martín. 2020. "From Spaces to Circuits of Extraction: Value in Process and the Mine/City Nexus." *Capitalism Nature Socialism* 31(3): 114–133. https://doi.org/10.1080/10455752.2019.1656758
Arroyo, Priscilla. 2020. "Multinacionais são financiadoras ocultas da Frente Parlamentar da Agropecuária." De olho nos ruralistas. Last Modified June 16, 2020. https://deolhonosruralistas.com.br/2019/05/21/multinacionais-sao-financiadoras-ocultas-da-frente-parlamentar-da-agropecuaria/
Artacker, Tamara, Jorge Campanini, and Eduardo Gudynas. 2020. "Extractivismos agropecuarios en tiempos de pandemia: flexibilizaciones, asimetrías, autoritarismos y otros efectos derrame." *Yeiyá* 1(1): 89–107. https://doi.org/10.33182/y.v1i1.1303
Assentamento SINOP. 1973. Foto aérea Acervo Fotográfico TenCelJaimeRibeiro. Last modified February 3, 2015. https://commons.wikimedia.org/wiki/File:1973Jul,BR163,ColonizacaoSINOP.jpg

Athayde, Simone, Mason Mathews, Stephanie Bohlman, Walterlina Brasil, Carolina RC Doria, Jynessa Dutka-Gianelli, Philip M. Fearnside, et al. 2019. "Mapping Research on Hydropower and Sustainability in the Brazilian Amazon: Advances, Gaps in Knowledge and Future Directions." *Current Opinion in Environmental Sustainability* 37: 50–69. https://doi.org/10.1016/j.cosust.2019.06.004

Banerjee, Bobby S. 2008. "Necrocapitalism." *Organization Studies* 29(12): 1541–1563. https://doi.org/10.1177/0170840607096386

Barbier, Edward B. 2012. "Scarcity, Frontiers and Development." *The Geographical Journal* 178(2): 110–22. https://doi.org/10.1111/j.1475-4959.2012.00462.x

Barbosa, Catarina. 2020. "Dia do fogo": um ano depois, só 5% dos culpados foram punidos." *Brasil de Fato* (São Paulo), August 10, 2020. https://www.brasildefato.com.br/2020/08/10/dia-do-fogo-um-ano-depois-so-5-dos-culpados-foram-punidos

BBC News. 2019. "Brazil's Bolsonaro says DiCaprio gave cash 'to set Amazon on fire.'" *BBC News (Latin America)*, November 30, 2019. bbc.com/news/world-latin-america-50613054

Bebbington, Anthony, Abdul-Gafaru Abdulai, Denise Humphreys Bebbington, Marja Hinfelaar, and Cynthia Sanborn. 2018. *Governing Extractive Industries: Politics, Histories, Ideas*. Oxford: Oxford University Press. https://doi.org/10.1093/oso/9780198820932.001.0001

Belcher, Oliver, Patrick Bigger, Ben Neimark, and Cara Kennelly. 2019. "Hidden Carbon Costs of the 'Everywhere War': Logistics, Geopolitical Ecology, and the Carbon Boot-Print of the US Military." *Transactions of the Institute of British Geographers* 45(1): 65–80. https://doi.org/10.1111/tran.12319

Berwyn, Bob. 2021. "Many Scientists Now Say Global Warming Could Stop Relatively Quickly After Emissions Go to Zero." *Inside Climate News*, January 3, 2021. https://insideclimatenews.org/news/03012021/five-aspects-climate-change-2020/

Blackman, Allen, Leonardo Corral, Eirivelthon Santos Lima, and Gregory P. Asner. 2017. "Titling indigenous communities protects forests in the Peruvian Amazon." *Proceedings of the National Academy of Sciences* 114: 4123–4128. https://doi.org/10.1073/pnas.1603290114

Blaser, Mario. 2009. "Political Ontology: *Cultural Studies without 'Cultures?'*" *Cultural Studies* 23(5–6): 873–96. https://doi.org/10.1080/09502380903208023

Blaser, Mario. 2010. *Storytelling Globalization from the Chaco and Beyond*. Durham, NC: Duke University Press.

Blaser, Mario. 2013. "Ontological Conflicts and the Stories of Peoples in Spite of Europe: Toward a Conversation on Political Ontology." *Current Anthropology* 54(5), 574–568. https://www.journals.uchicago.edu/doi/10.1086/672270

Blodget, Henry. 2011. "Jeremy Grantham: We're Headed for a Disaster of Biblical Proportions," *Insider*, June 13, 2011. https://www.businessinsider.com/jeremy-grantham-commodity-prices-2011-6?r=US&IR=T

Bond, Patrick. 2006. *Looting Africa: The Economics of Exploitation*. London: Zed Books.

Borras, Saturnino M. Jr., Jennifer C. Franco, S. Ryan Isakson, Les Levidow, and Pietje Verves. 2016. "The Rise of Flex Crops and Commodities: Implications for Research." *The Journal of Peasant Studies* 43(1): 93–115. https://doi.org/10.1080/03066150.2015.1036417

Borras, Saturnino M. Jr., Jennifer C. Franco, Sergio Gómez, Cristóbal Kay, and Max Spoor. 2012. "Land Grabbing in Latin America and the Caribbean." *The Journal of Peasant Studies* 39(3–4): 845–872. https://doi.org/10.1080/03066150.2012.679931

Borras, Saturnino M. Jr., Ruth Hall, Ian Scoones, Ben N. F. White, and Wendy Wolford. 2011. "Towards a Better Understanding of Global Land Grabbing: An Editorial Introduction." *The Journal of Peasant Studies* 38(2): 209–216. https://doi.org/10.1080/03066150.2011.559005

Bourdieu, Pierre. 1991. *Language and Symbolic Power*. Cambridge, UK: Polity Press.

Boivin, Nicole, and Alison Crowther. 2021. "Mobilizing the Past to Shape a Better Anthropocene." *Nature Ecology & Evolution* 5: 273–284. https://doi.org/10.1038/s41559-020-01361-4

Bowman Maria S., Britaldo S. Soares-Filho, Frank D. Merry, Daniel C. Nepstas, Hermann Rodrigues, and Oriana T. Almeida. 2012. "Persistence of Cattle Ranching in the Brazilian Amazon: A Spatial Analysis of the Rationale for Beef Production." *Land Use Policy* 29(3): 558–568. https://doi.org/10.1016/j.landusepol.2011.09.009

Bradshaw, Corey J. A., Paul R. Ehrlich, Andrew Beattie, Gerardo Ceballos, Eileen Crist, Joan Diamond, Rodolfo Dirzo, et al. 2021. "Underestimating the Challenges of Avoiding a Ghastly Future." *Frontiers in Conservation Science* 1(9). https://doi.org/10.3389/fcosc.2020.615419

Brasil 247. 2013. "MST compara Dilma a Geisel e avisa: vai radicalizar," *Brasil 247,* September 17, 2013. http://www.brasil247.com/pt/247/brasil/115233/

Broad, Robin, and John Cavanagh. 2021. *The Water Defenders: How Ordinary People Saved a Country from Corporate Greed*. Boston, MA: Beacon Press.

Browder, John O., Marcos A. Pedlowski, Robert Walker, Randolph H. Wynne, Percy M. Summers, Ana Abad, Nancy Becerra-Cordoba, and Joao Mil-Homens. 2008. "Revisiting Theories of Frontier Expansion in the Brazilian Amazon: A Survey of the Colonist Farming Population in Rondônia's Post-Frontier, 1992–2002." *World Development* 36(8): 1469–1492. https://doi.org/10.1016/j.worlddev.2007.08.008

Brum, Eliane. 2014. "Belo Monte: a anatomia de um etnocídio." *El País*, December 1, 2014. https://brasil.elpais.com/brasil/2014/12/01/opinion/1417437633_930086.html

Bryan, Bob. 2016. "Jeremy Grantham publishes epic mea culpa admitting he got the commodities bubble all wrong," *Insider*, May 10, 2016. 2021 from https://www.businessinsider.com/jeremy-grantham-admits-he-was-wrong-2016-5?r=US&IR=T

Bunker, Stephen G. 1985. *Underdeveloping the Amazon: Extraction, Unequal Exchange, and the Failure of the Modern State*. Chicago, IL: University of Chicago Press.

Bunker, Stephen G., and Paul S. Ciccantell. 2006. *Globalization and the Race for Resources*. Baltimore, MD: Johns Hopkins University Press.

Camilleri, Joseph A., and Jim Falk. 2009. *Worlds in Transition: Evolving Governance across a Stressed Planet*. Cheltenham, UK: Edward Elgar.

Caretta, Martina Angela, and Sofia Zaragocin. 2020. "Women's Resistance Against the Extractive Industry: Embodied and Water Dimensions." *Human Geography* 13(1): 3–5. https://doi.org/10.1177/1942778620910893

Carney, Judith A. 2020. "Subsistence in the Plantationocene: Dooryard Gardens, Agrobiodiversity, and the Subaltern Economies of Slavery" *The Journal of Peasant Studies*: 1–25 (ahead-of-print). https://doi.org/10.1080/03066150.2020.1725488

Carter, Miguel, ed. 2015. *Challenging Social Inequality: The Landless Rural Workers Movement and Agrarian Reform in Brazil*. Durham, NC: Duke University Press.

Ceballos, Gerardo, Paul R. Ehrlich, and Peter H. Raven. 2020. "Vertebrates on the Brink as Indicators of Biological Annihilation and the Sixth Mass Extinction." *Proceedings of the National Academy of Sciences* 117(24): 13596–13602. https://doi.org/10.1073/pnas.1922686117

Chagnon, Christopher W., Sophia Hagolani-Albov, and Saana M. Hokkanen. 2021. "Extractivism at Your Fingertips." In *Our Extractive Age: Expressions of Violence and Resistance*, edited by Judith Shapiro and John-Allen McNeish. London, UK: Routledge (ahead-of-print).

Chanchosa, Blanca. 2021. "Climate Emergency and Species Extinction – Resist! Construct! Celebrate!" World Social Forum 2021. Streamed live on Jan 29, 2021, YouTube Video 1:50:46. https://youtu.be/jpAE2Hifbi0.

Clapp, Jennifer. 2021. "Explaining Growing Glyphosate Use: The Political Economy of Herbicide-Dependent Agriculture." *Global Environmental Change* 67(102239): 1–11. https://doi.org/10.1016/j.gloenvcha.2021.102239

Cleary, David. 1993. "After the Frontier: Problems with Political Economy in the Modern Brazilian Amazon." *Journal of Latin American Studies* 25(2): 331–49. https://www.jstor.org/stable/158160

Clements, Elizabeth Alice, and Bernardo Mançano Fernandes. 2013. "Land Grabbing, Agribusiness and the Peasantry in Brazil and Mozambique." *Agrarian South: Journal of Political Economy* 2(1): 41–69. https://doi.org/10.1177/2277976013477185

Colli, Guarino R., Cecília R. Vieira, and José Carmine Dianese. 2020. "Biodiversity and Conservation of the Cerrado: Recent Advances and Old Challenges." *Biodiversity and Conservation* 29: 1465–1475. https://doi.org/10.1007/s10531-020-01967-x

Collins Randall. 2013. "The End of Middle-Class Work: No More Escapes." In *Does capitalism have a future?*, edited by Immanuel Wallerstein, Randall Collins, Michael Mann, Georgi Derluguian, and Craig Calhoun. 37–70. Oxford, UK: Oxford University Press.

Cortés-McPherson, Dolores. 2019. "Expansion of Small-Scale Gold Mining in Madre de Dios: 'Capital Interests' and the Emergence of a New Elite of Entrepreneurs in the Peruvian Amazon." *The Extractive Industries and Society* 6(2): 382–389.

Covey, Kristofer, Fiona Soper, Sunitha Pangala, Angelo Bernardino, Zoe Pagliaro, Luana Basso, Henrique Cassol, et al. 2021. "Carbon and Beyond: The Biogeochemistry of Climate in a Rapidly Changing Amazon." *Frontiers in Forests and Global Change* 4:618401. https://doi.org/10.3389/ffgc.2021.618401

Cummings, Claire H. 2008. *Uncertain Peril: Genetic Engineering and the Future of Seeds*. Boston, MA: Beacon Press.

Danowski Déborah, and Eduardo Viveiros de Castro. 2017. *The Ends of the World*. Cambridge, UK: Polity Press.

de Area Leão Pereira, Eder Johnson, Luiz Carlos de Santana Ribeiro, Lúcio Flávio da Silva Freitas, and Hernane Borges de Barros Pereira. 2020. "Brazilian Policy and Agribusiness Damage the Amazon Rainforest." *Land Use Policy* 92:104491. https://doi.org/10.1016/j.landusepol.2020.104491

de la Cadena, Marisol. 2010. "Indigenous Cosmopolitics in the Andes: Conceptual Reflections Beyond 'Politics.'" *Cultural Anthropology* 25(2): 334–370. https://doi.org/10.1111/j.1548-1360.2010.01061.x

de la Cadena, Marisol. 2015. *Earth Beings: Ecologies of Practice Across Andean Worlds*. Durham, NC: Duke University Press.

de la Cadena, Marisol. 2020. "Protesting from the uncommons." In *Indigenous Women and Climate Change*, edited by Rocío Silva-Santisteban. 35–42. Lima, Peru: IWGIA.

de la Cadena, Marisol, and Mario Blaser, eds. 2018. *A World of Many Worlds*. Durham, NC: Duke University Press.

de Souza Mendes, Flávia, Daniel Baron, Gerhard Gerold, Veraldo Liesenberg, and Stefan Erasmi. 2019. "Optical and SAR Remote Sensing Synergism for Mapping Vegetation Types in the Endangered Cerrado/Amazon Ecotone of Nova Mutum—Mato Grosso." *Remote Sensing* 11(10): 1161. https://doi.org/10.3390/rs11101161

de Toledo, Peter Mann, Eloi Dalla-Nora, Ima Célia Guimarães Vieira, Ana Paula Dutra Aguiar, and Roberto Araújo. 2017. "Development Paradigms Contributing to the Transformation of the Brazilian Amazon: Do People Matter?" *Current Opinion in Environmental Sustainability* 26–27: 77–83. https://doi.org/10.1016/j.cosust.2017.01.009

dos Santos, Gilberto Vieira. 2020. "Governo Bolsonaro: o retorno da velha política genocida indígena." *Revista da ANPEGE* 16(29): 420–451. https://doi.org/10.5418/ra2020.v16i29.12527

Domingues, Mariana Soares, and Célio Bermann. 2012. "O arco de desflorestamentos na Amazônia: Da pecuária à soja." *Ambiente e Sociedade* 15(2): 1–22. http://dx.doi.org/10.1590/S1414-753X2012000200002

Dowbor, Ladislau. 2019. *The Age of Unproductive Capital: New Architectures of Power*. Newcastle upon Tyne, UK: Cambridge Scholars.

Dunlap, Alexander. 2020. "The Politics of Ecocide, Genocide and Megaprojects: Interrogating Natural Resource Extraction, Identity and the Normalization of Erasure." *Journal of Genocide Research*, 1–24. https://doi.org/10.1080/14623528.2020.1754051

Dunlap, Alexander, and Jostein Jakobsen. 2020. *The Violent Technologies of Extraction: Political Ecology, Critical Agrarian Studies and the Capitalist*

*Worldeater*. London, UK: Palgrave Pivot. https://doi.org/10.1007/978-3-030-26852-7

Durante, Francesco, Markus Kröger, and William LaFleur. 2021. "Extraction and extractivisms: definitions and concepts." In *Our Extractive Age: Expressions of Violence and Resistance*, edited by Judith Shapiro and John-Allen McNeish. Ahead-of-Print. London, UK: Routledge.

Edelman Marc, Carlos Oya, and Saturnino M. Borras Jr. 2013. "Global Land Grabs: Historical Processes, Theoretical and Methodological Implications and Current Trajectories." *Third World Quarterly* 34: 1517–31. https://doi.org/10.1080/01436597.2013.850190

Ehrnström-Fuentes, Maria. 2019. "Confronting extractivism–the role of local struggles in the (un)making of place." In *Critical Perspectives on International Business*. Vol. ahead-of-print No. ahead-of-print. https://doi.org/10.1108/cpoib-01-2018-0016

Ehrnström-Fuentes, Maria. 2020. "Organising in Defence of Life: The Emergence and Dynamics of a Territorial Movement in Southern Chile." *Organization*. https://doi.org/10.1177/1350508420963871

Ehrnström-Fuentes, Maria, and Markus Kröger. 2017. "In the Shadows of Social Licence to Operate: Untold Investment Grievances in Latin America." *Journal of Cleaner Production* 141: 346–358, https://doi.org/10.1016/j.jclepro.2016.09.112

Ehrnström-Fuentes, Maria, and Markus Kröger, 2018. "Birthing Extractivism: The Role of the State in Forestry Politics and Development in Uruguay." *Journal of Rural Studies* 57: 197–208. https://doi.org/10.1016/j.jrurstud.2017.12.022

Elonen, Piia. 2019. "Brasilian sademetsien ja Suomen kuukkelien kohtalo ei jättänyt rauhaan." *Climate Correspondent* (blog)." *Helsingin Sanomat*, October 28, 2019. https://www.hs.fi/blogi/ilmastokirjeenvaihtaja/art-2000006284897.html

Eloy, Ludivine, Catherine Aubertin, Fabiano Toni, Silvia Laine Borges Lúcio, and Marion Bosgiraud. 2016. "On the Margins of Soy Farms: Traditional Populations and Selective Environmental Policies in the Brazilian Cerrado." *The Journal of Peasant Studies* 43(2): 494–516. https://doi.org/10.1080/03066150.2015.1013099

Engels, Bettina. 2021. "All Good Things Come From Below? Scalar Constructions of the 'Local' in Conflicts Over Mining." *Political Geography* 84. https://doi.org/10.1016/j.polgeo.2020.102295

Escobar, Arturo. 2016. "Sentipensar con la Tierra: Las Luchas Territoriales y la Dimensión Ontológica de las Epistemologías del Sur." *AIBR, Revista de Antropología Iberoamericana* 11(01): 11–32.

Escobar, Arturo. 2020. *Pluriversal Politics: The Real and the Possible*. Durham, NC: Duke University Press.

Escobar, Arturo. 2021. *Encountering Development: The Making and Unmaking of the Third World*. Princeton, NJ: Princeton University Press.

Eufemia, Luca, Hector Morales, Michelle Bonatti, Maximilian Graser, Marcos Lana, and Stefan Sieber. 2019. "Collective Perception of Anthropic and Extractive Interventions in the Colombian Llanos." *Social Sciences* 8(9): 259. https://doi.org/10.3390/socsci8090259

EurActiv, 2021. "Mining Fuels Greenland Dreams of Independence – and Political Crisis," *Euractiv.com with AFP*. February 17, 2021. https://www.euractiv.com/section/politics/news/mining-fuels-greenland-dreams-of-independence-and-political-crisis/

Fearnside, Phillip M. 2008. "The Roles and Movements of Actors in the Deforestation of Brazilian Amazonia." *Ecology and Society* 13(1): 23. http://www.jstor.org/stable/26267941

Fernandes, Bernardo Mançano. 2009. "The MST and Agrarian Reform in Brazil." *Socialism and Democracy* 23(3): 90–99. https://doi.org/10.1080/08854300903155541

Finnish Ministry of Foreign Affairs. 2021. "Recommendations to Finland on the Implementation of Economic, Social and Cultural Rights." Press Release. March 8, 2021. https://valtioneuvosto.fi/en/-/recommendations-to-finland-on-the-implementation-of-economic-social-and-cultural-rights

Foster, John B. 1999. "Marx's Theory of Metabolic Rift : Classical Foundations for Environmental Sociology." *The American Journal of Sociology* 105(2): 366–405. https://doi.org/10.1086/210315

Foweraker, Joe. 1981. *The Struggle for Land: A Political Economy of the Pioneer Frontier in Brazil from 1930 to the Present Day*. Cambridge, UK: Cambridge University Press.

Frank, Andre Gunder, and Barry Gills. 1993. *The World System: Five Hundred Years or Five Thousand?* New York, NY: Routledge.

Freshour, Carrie. 2019. "Cheap meat and cheap work in the U.S. poultry industry: race, gender, and immigration in corporate strategies to shape labor." In *Global Meat: Social and Environmental Consequences of the Expanding Meat Industry*, edited by Bill Winders and Elizabeth Ransom. 121–140. Cambridge, MA: MIT Press.

Gan, Elaine, Nils Bubandt, Anna Lowenhaupt Tsing, and Heather Anne Swanson. 2017. "Introduction: Haunted landscapes of the anthropocene." In *Arts of Living on a Damaged Planet: Ghosts and Monsters of the Anthropocene*, edited by Anna Lowenhaupt Tsing, Heather Anne Swanson, Elaine Gan, and Nils Bubandt. G1–G14. Minneapolis, MN: University of Minnesota Press.

Garrett, Rachael D., and Lisa L. Rausch. 2016. "Green for Gold: Social and Ecological Tradeoffs Influencing the Sustainability of the Brazilian Soy Industry." *The Journal of Peasant Studies* 43(2): 461–493. https://doi.org/10.1080/03066150.2015.1010077

Gills, Barry, and Jamie Morgan. 2020. "Global Climate Emergency: After COP24, Climate Science, Urgency, and the Threat to Humanity." *Globalizations* 17(6): 885–902. https://doi.org/10.1080/14747731.2019.1669915

Giovanaz, Daniel. 2020. "How Bolsonaro's Pro-Pesticide Policy Transfers Wealth Out of the Country," *Brasil de Fato* (São Paulo) December 16, 2020. https://www.brasildefato.com.br/2020/12/16/how-bolsonaro-s-pro-pesticide-policy-transfers-wealth-outside-of-the-country

Gomez-Pereira, Jonathan. 2020. "The Altar of National Prosperity: Extractivism and Sacrifice Zones in Argentine Patagonia." *Anthropology Department Honors Papers* 18. https://digitalcommons.conncoll.edu/anthrohp/18

González, Nidia Catherine, and Kröger, Markus. 2020. "The Potential of Amazon Indigenous Agroforestry Practices and Ontologies for Rethinking Global Forest Governance." *Forest Policy and Economics* 118: 102257. https://doi.org/10.1016/j.forpol.2020.102257

González-Hidalgo, Marien, Sandra López-Dietz, and Stefanie Pacheco-Pailahual. 2019. "El sentipensar extractivo colonial: Geografías emocionales de la extracción en Gülumapu, el territorio mapuche en el sur de Chile." *Journal of Latin American Geography* 18(3): 85–109. https://doi.org/10.1353/lag.2019.0055

Grosfoguel, Ramón. 2011. "Decolonizing Post-Colonial Studies and Paradigms of Political-Economy: Transmodernity, Decolonial Thinking, and Global Coloniality." *Transmodernity: Journal of Peripheral Cultural Production of the Luso-Hispanic World* 1(1). https://escholarship.org/uc/item/21k6t3fq

Grosfoguel, Ramón. 2016. "Del 'extractivismo económico' al 'extractivismo epistémico' y 'extractivismo ontológico': una forma destructiva de conocer, ser y estar en el mundo." *Tabula Rasa* 24: 123–143.

Gudynas, Eduardo. 2009. "La ecología política del giro biocéntrico en la nueva Constitución de Ecuador." *Revista de estudios sociales* 32: 34–47. http://journals.openedition.org/revestudsoc/16260

Gudynas, Eduardo. 2015. *Extractivismos. Ecología, economía y política de un modo de entender el desarrollo y la Naturaleza*. Cochabamba, Bolivua: CEDIB/CLAES.

Gudynas, Eduardo. 2017. "Value, Growth, Development: South American Lessons for a New Ecopolitics." *Capitalism Nature Socialism* 32(2): 234–243. https://doi.org/10.1080/10455752.2017.1372502

Gudynas, Eduardo. 2020a. "Opening Plenary Roundtable Discussion." Global Extractivisms and Alternatives Initiative (EXALT) 2020 Symposium. October 21, 2021 [Online]. YouTube Video 1:55:51. https://youtu.be/7XMMyyv_bSQ

Gudynas, Eduardo. 2020b. *Tan cerca y tan lejos de las alternativas al desarrollo. Planes, programas y pactos en tiempos de pandemia*. Lima, Peru: RedGE y CooperAcción.

Gudynas, Eduardo. 2021. *Extractivisms. Politics, Economy and Ecology*. Black Point, Canada: Fernwood Publishing.

Guzmán-Gallegos, María A. 2019. "Controlling abandoned oil installations: Ruination and ownership in Northern Peruvian Amazonia." In *Indigenous Life Projects and Extractivism. Approaches to Social Inequality and Difference*, edited by Cecilie Vindal Ødegaard and Juan Javier Rivera Andía, 53–73. London, UK: Palgrave McMillian.

Hanski, Ilkka. 2000. "Extinction Debt and Species Credit in Boreal Forests: Modelling the Consequences of Different Approaches to Biodiversity Conservation." *Annales Zoologici Fennici* 37(4): 271–280. http://www.jstor.org/stable/23735720

Haraway, Donna. 2004. *The Haraway Reader*. New York, NY: Routledge.

Haraway, Donna. 2015. "Anthropocene, Capitalocene, Plantationocene, Chthulucene: Making Kin." *Environmental humanities* 6(1): 159–165. https://doi.org/10.1215/22011919-3615934

Haraway, Donna, Noburo Ishikawa, Scott F. Gilbert, Kenneth Olwig, Anna L. Tsing, and Nils Bubandt. 2016. "Anthropologists Are Talking - About the Anthropocene." *Ethnos* 81(3): 535–564. https://doi.org/10.1080/00141844.2015.1105838

Harvey, David. 2005. *The New Imperialism*. Oxford, UK: Oxford University Press.

Harvey, Fiona. 2019. "Europe Must Act on Intensive Farming to Save Wildlife, Scientists Say," *The Guardian*. November 5, 2019. https://www.theguardian.com/environment/2019/nov/05/europe-must-act-on-intensive-farming-to-save-wildlife-scientists-say

Hay, Colin. 2006. "Political ontology." In *The Oxford Handbook of Contextual Political Analysis (Online)*, edited by Robert E. Goodin and Charles Tilly. Oxford, UK: Oxford University Press. https://doi.org/10.1093/oxfordhb/9780199270439.003.0004

He, Meddy. 2013. "Cargill Inaugurates Integrated Poultry Operation in Lai'an, Anhui." Cargill. September 23, 2013. https://www.cargill.com/news/releases/2013/NA3077688.jsp

Healy, Noel, Jennie C. Stephens, and Stephanie A. Malin. 2019. "Embodied Energy Injustices: Unveiling and Politicizing the Transboundary Harms of Fossil Fuel Extractivism and Fossil Fuel Supply Chains." *Energy Research & Social Science* 48: 219–234. https://doi.org/10.1016/j.erss.2018.09.016

Hecht, Susanna B. 2005. "Soybeans, Development and Conservation on the Amazon Frontier." *Development and Change* 36(2): 375–404. https://doi.org/10.1111/j.0012-155X.2005.00415.x

Hecht, Susanna B. 2011. "From Eco-Catastrophe to Zero Deforestation? Interdisciplinarities, Politics, Environmentalisms and Reduced Clearing in Amazonia." *Environmental Conservation* 39(1): 4–19. https://doi.org/10.1017/S0376892911000452

Hecht, Susanna B., and Alexander Cockburn. 1989. *Fate of the Forest: Developers, Destroyers, and Defenders of the Amazon*. London, UK: Verso.

Henderson, Caspar. 2014. "The Sixth Extinction by Elizabeth Kolbert – Review," *The Guardian*. February 14, 2014. https://www.theguardian.com/books/2014/feb/14/sixth-extinction-unnatural-history-kolbert-review

Higgins, Polly Damien Short, and Nigel South, 2013. "Protecting the Planet: A Proposal for a Law Ecocide." *Crime Law and Social Change* 59(3): 251–266. https://doi.org/10.1007/s10611-013-9413-6

Higgins, Tiffany, 2020. "Belo Monte boondoggle: Brazil's Biggest, Costliest Dam May be Unviable." Mongabay Series: Amazon Infrastructure. January 17, 2020. https://news.mongabay.com/2020/01/belo-monte-boondoggle-brazils-biggest-costliest-dam-may-be-unviable/

Hochstetler, Kathryn, and Margaret E. Keck. 2007. *Greening Brazil: Environmental Activism in State and Society*. Durham, NC: Duke University Press.

Holland, Lynn. 2020. "Illegal Gold Mining and the Struggle to Save the Amazon in Peru." In *Frontiers of Development in the Amazon: Riches, Risks, and Resistances*, edited by Antonio Augusto Rossotto Ioris, Rafael R. Ioris, and Sergei Shubin. 189–212. Lanham, MD: Lexington Books.

Hornborg, Alf. 2011. *Global Ecology and Unequal Exchange: Fetishism in a Zero-Sum World*. London, UK: Routledge. https://doi.org/10.4324/9780203806890

Hougaard, Inge-Merete, and Irene Vélez-Torres. 2020. "Shifting Sands: Legal Dispossession of Small-Scale Miners in an Extractivist Era." *Geoforum* 115: 81–89. https://doi.org/10.1016/j.geoforum.2020.06.022

Huseman, Jennifer, and Damien Short. 2012. "'A Slow Industrial Genocide': Tar Sands and the Indigenous Peoples of Northern Alberta." *International Journal of Human Rights* 16(1): 216–37. https://doi.org/10.1080/13642987.2011.649593

Hyvärinen, Pieta. 2020. "Sienestystä pohjoisilla puupelloilla: metsien moninaiset taloudet ja plantaasiosentrismin ongelma." *Alue ja Ympäristö* 49(2): 22–43. https://doi.org/10.30663/ay.97101

Ingold, Tim. 2008. "Bindings Against Boundaries: Entanglements of Life in an Open World." *Environment and Planning A: Economy and Space* 40(8): 1796–1810. https://doi.org/10.1068/a40156

Ioris, Antonio Augusto Rossotto. 2017. *Agribusiness and the Neoliberal Food System in Brazil: Frontiers and Fissures of Agro-Neoliberalism*. Oxfordshire, UK: Routledge.

Ioris, Antonio Augusto Rossotto. 2020. *Kaiowcídio: Genocídio Guarani-Kaiowá*. Cardiff, UK: Cardiff University. ISBN: 9798694474726

IPBES. 2019a. *Global Assessment Report on Biodiversity and Ecosystem Services of the Intergovernmental Science-Policy Platform on Biodiversity and Ecosystem Services*, edited by Eduardo Brondízio, Josef Settele, Sandra Díaz, and Hien T. Ngo (eds). Bonn, Germany: IPBES Secretariat.

IPBES. 2019b. *Chapter 2.2 of the IPBES Global Assessment on Biodiversity and Ecosystem Services: Status and Trends – Nature (Draft)*. Authors Nakul Chettri, Ehsan Dulloo, Andrew Hendry, Bardukh Gabrielyan, Julian Gutt, Ute Jacob, Emre Keskin, et al. https://ipbes.net/sites/default/files/ipbes_global_assessment_chapter_2_2_nature_unedited_31may.pdf

Isomäki, Risto. 2021. *Mitä koronapandemian jälkeen*. Helsinki, Finland: Into Kustannus.

Jalbert, Kirk, Anna Willow, David Casagrande, and Stephanie Paladino, eds. 2017. *ExtrACTION: Impacts, Engagements, and Alternative Futures*. New York, NY: Routledge.

Jepson, Wendy. 2006. "Producing a Modern Agricultural Frontier: Firms and Cooperatives in Eastern Matto Grosso, Brazil." *Economic Geography* 82(3): 289–316. https://doi.org/10.1111/j.1944-8287.2006.tb00312.x

Kenney-Lazar, Miles, and Noboru Ishikawa. 2019. "Mega-Plantations in Southeast Asia: Landscapes of Displacement." *Environment and Society* 10(1): 63–82. https://doi.org/10.3167/ares.2019.100105

Kimmerer, Robin Wall. 2017. "Learning the Grammar of Animacy." *Anthropology of Consciousness* 28(2): 128–134. https://doi.org/10.1111/anoc.12081

Klare, Michael T. 2019. *All Hell Breaking Loose: The Pentagon's Perspective on Climate Change*. New York, NY: Henry Holt.

Kohn, Eduardo. 2013. *How Forests Think: Toward an Anthropology Beyond the Human*. Berkeley, CA: University of California Press.

Kopenawa, Davi, and Bruce Albert. 2013. *The Falling Sky*. Cambridge, MA: Harvard University Press.

Koponen, Juhani, and Sakari Saaritsa, eds. 2019. *Nälkämaasta hyvinvointivaltioksi: Suomi kehityksen kiinniottajana*. Helsinki, Finland: Gaudeamus.

Kothari, Ashish, Ariel Salleh, Arturo Escobar, Federico Demaria, and Alberto Acosta, eds. 2019. *Pluriverse: A Post-Development Dictionary*. New Delhi, India: Tulika Books.

Kotiaho Janne S. 2017. "On Effective Biodiversity Conservation, Sustainability of Bioeconomy, and Honesty of the Finnish Forest Policy." *Annales Zoologici Fennici* 54(1/4): 13–25. https://doi.org/10.5735/086.054.0104

Kröger, Markus. 2011. "Promotion of Contentious Agency as a Rewarding Movement Strategy: Evidence From the MST-Paper Industry Conflicts in Brazil." *The Journal of Peasant Studies* 38(2): 435–458. https://doi.org/10.1080/03066150.2011.559016

Kröger, Markus. 2012. "Neo-Mercantilist Capitalism and Post-2008 Cleavages in Economic Decision-Making Power in Brazil." *Third World Quarterly* 33(5): 887–901. https://doi.org/10.1080/01436597.2012.674703

Kröger, Markus. 2013a. *Contentious Agency and Natural Resource Politics*. London, UK: Routledge.

Kröger, Markus. 2013b. "Globalization as the 'Pulping' of Landscapes: Forestry Capitalism's North–South Territorial Accumulation." *Globalizations* 10(6): 837–853. https://doi.org/10.1080/14747731.2013.814433

Kröger, Markus. 2013c. "Grievances, Agency and the Absence of Conflict: The New Suzano Pulp Investment in the Eastern Amazon." *Forest Policy and Economics* 33, 28–35. https://doi.org/10.1016/j.forpol.2013.02.005

Kröger, Markus. 2014. "The Political Economy of Global Tree Plantation Expansion: A Review." *The Journal of Peasant Studies* 41(2): 235–261. https://doi.org/10.1080/03066150.2014.890596

Kröger, Markus. 2016a. "Spatial Causalities in Resource Rushes: Notes from the Finnish Mining Boom." *Journal of Agrarian Change* 16(4): 543–570. https://doi.org/10.1111/joac.12113

Kröger, Markus. 2016b. "The Political Economy of 'Flex Trees': A Preliminary Analysis." *The Journal of Peasant Studies* 43(4): 886–909. https://doi.org/10.1080/03066150.2016.1140646

Kröger, Markus. 2017. "Inter-Sectoral Determinants of Forest Policy: The Power of Deforesting Actors In Post-2012 Brazil." *Forest Policy and Economics* 77: 24–32. https://doi.org/10.1016/j.forpol.2016.06.003

Kröger, Markus. 2018. "The New 'Sustainable Communitarian' Logging Schemes and Their Critique Inside Multiple-Use Conservation Areas in the Brazilian Amazon: Preliminary Notes." *Globalizations* 15(5): 581–592. https://doi.org/10.1080/14747731.2018.1474032

Kröger, Markus. 2019a. "The global land rush and the arctic." In *The GlobalArctic Handbook*, edited by Mattias Finger and Lassi Heininen, 27–43. New York, NY: Springer, Cham.

Kröger, Markus. 2019b. "O crescimento acelerado e o colapso do extrativismo do minério de ferro: o nexo Brasil-Índia-China." In *Desenvolvimento*

*E Transformações Agrárias: Brics, competição e cooperação no Sul Global*, edited by Sérgio Sauer, 307–324. São Paulo, Brazil: Outras Expressões.

Kröger, Markus. 2020a. *Iron Will: Global Extractivism and Mining Resistance in Brazil and India*. Ann Arbor, MI: Michigan University Press. https://doi.org/10.3998/mpub.11533186

Kröger, Markus. 2020b. *Politics of Extraction: Theories and New Concepts for Critical Analysis*. Oxford Bibliographies Online in International Relations. https://doi.org/10.1093/obo/9780199743292-0292

Kröger, Markus. 2020c. *Natural Resources, Energy Politics, and Environmental Consequences*. Oxford Bibliographies Online in International Relations. https://doi.org/10.1093/obo/9780199743292-0291

Kröger, Markus. 2020d. "Deforestation, Cattle Capitalism and Neodevelopmentalism in the Chico Mendes Extractive Reserve, Brazil." *The Journal of Peasant Studies* 47 (3): 464–482. https://doi.org/10.1080/03066150.2019.1604510

Kröger, Markus. 2021. *Studying Complex Interactions and Outcomes Through Qualitative Comparative Analysis: A Practical Guide to Comparative Case Studies and Ethnographic Data Analysis*. London, UK: Routledge.

Kröger, Markus, and Maria Ehrnström-Fuentes. 2021. "Forestry extractivism" In *Agrarian Extractivism in Latin America*, edited by Ben M. McKay, A. Alonso-Fradejas, and A. Ezquerro-Cañete. London, UK: Routledge.

Kröger, Markus, and Rickard Lalander. 2016. "Ethnic-Territorial Rights and the Resource Extraction Boom in Latin America: Do Constitutions Matter?" *Third World Quarterly* 37(4): 682–702. https://doi.org/10.1080/01436597.2015.1127154

Kröger, Markus, and Jan-Erik Nylund 2012. "The Conflict over Veracel Pulpwood Plantations in Brazil—Application of Ethical Analysis." *Forest Policy and Economics* 14(1): 74–82. https://doi.org/10.1016/j.forpol.2011.07.018

Kröger, Markus, and Anja Nygren. 2020. "Shifting Frontier Dynamics in Latin America." *Journal of Agrarian Change* 20(3): 364–386. https://doi.org/10.1111/joac.12354

Kröger, Markus, and Raitio, Kaisa. 2017. "Finnish Forest Policy in the Era of Bioeconomy: A Pathway to Sustainability?" *Forest Policy and Economics* 77: 6–15. https://doi.org/10.1016/j.forpol.2016.12.003

Kuisma, Markku. 2006. *Metsäteollisuuden maa: Suomi, metsät ja kansainvälinen järjestelmä*. Helsinki, Finland: SKS.

Kuokkanen, Rauna. 2017. "The Pursuit of Inuit Sovereignty in Greenland." *Northern Public Affairs* 5(2): 46–49. https://ssrn.com/abstract=3625831

Lassila Maija. 2020. "The Arctic Mineral Resource Rush and the Ontological Struggle for the Viiankiaapa Peatland in Sodankylä, Finland." *Globalizations* 18(4): 635–649. https://doi.org/10.1080/14747731.2020.1831818

Lazzarini, Sergio G. 2011. *Capitalismo de laços: Os donos de Brasil e suas conexões*. Rio de Janeiro, Brazil: Elsevier.

Leahy, Joe. 2017 "Temer Pushes Amazon Deforestation Bill in Brazil," *Financial Times*, July 18, 2017, Brazil. https://www.ft.com/content/1435c6ae-6b6a-11e7-bfeb-33fe0c5b7eaa

Leifsen, Ebsen. 2020. "The Socionature That Neo-Extractivism can see: Practicing Redistribution and Compensation Around Large-Scale Mining in the Southern Ecuadorian Amazon." *Political Geography* 82: 82102249. https://doi.org/10.1016/j.polgeo.2020.102249

Letonsaari, Tomi. (2009) "Metsänhaltijat itäsuomalaisessa kansanuskonnossa [Forest Spirits in Eastern Finnish Folk Religion]" (master's thesis, University of Jyväskylä, 2009).http://urn.fi/URN:NBN:fi:jyu-200907011757

Li, Tania Murray. 2010. "To Make Live or Let Die? Rural Dispossession and the Protection of Surplus Populations." *Antipode* 41(s1): 66–93. https://doi.org/10.1111/j.1467-8330.2009.00717.x

Li, Fabiana. 2015. *Unearthing Conflict: Corporate Mining, Activism, and Expertise in Peru*. Durham, NC: Duke University Press. https://doi.org/10.1215/9780822375869

Lila, Luana. 2015. "As veias abertas da Amazônia – Parte I." *Greenpeace* (blog). May 11, 2015. https://www.greenpeace.org/brasil/blog/as-veias-abertas-da-amazonia-parte-i/

Lima, Mendelson, Carlos Augusto Peres, Mark Ilan Abrahams, Carlos Antonio da Silva Junior, Gerlane de Medeiros Costa, and Reginaldo Carvalho dos Santos. 2019. "The Paradoxical Situation of the White-Lipped Peccary (Tayassu Pecari) in the State of Mato Grosso, Brazil." *Perspectives in Ecology and Conservation* 17(1): 36–39. https://doi.org/10.1016/j.pecon.2018.12.001

Lima, Mendelson, Carlos Antonio da Silva Junior, Lisa Rausch, Holly K. Gibbs, and Jerry Adriani Johann. 2019. "Demystifying sustainable soy in Brazil." *Land Use Policy* 82: 349–352. https://doi.org/10.1016/j.landusepol.2018.12.016

Lindgren, Tim. 2018. "Ecocide, Genocide and the Disregard of Alternative Life-Systems." *The International Journal of Human Rights* 22(4): 525–549. https://doi.org/10.1080/13642987.2017.1397631

Livingston, Julie. 2019. *Self-Devouring Growth: A Planetary Parable as Told from Southern Africa*. Durham, NC: Duke University Press.

Lovejoy Thomas E., and Carlos Nobre 2019. "Amazon Tipping Point: Last Chance for Action." *Science Advances* 5(12): eaba2949. https://doi.org/10.1126/sciadv.aba2949

Lyra, Mariana Galvão. 2019. "Challenging Extractivism: Activism Over the Aftermath of the Fundão Disaster." *The Extractive Industries and Society* 6(3): 897–905. https://doi.org/10.1016/j.exis.2019.05.010

Mann, Michael. 2013. "The end may be nigh, but for whom?" In *Docs Capitalism Have a Future?,* edited by Immanuel Wallerstein, Randall Collins, Michael Mann, Georgi Derluguian, and Craig Calhoun. 71–98. New York, NY: Oxford University Press.

Mann, Michael. 2021. *The New Climate War: The Fight to Take Back Our Planet*. New York, NY: PublicAffairs.

Mansur, Alexandre. 2017. "Desmatamento do Cerrado," *Época*, May 29, 2017. http://epoca.globo.com/tudo-sobre/noticia/2017/05/desmatamento-do-cerrado.html

Marchak, M. Patricia. 1995. *Logging the Globe*. Montreal, Canada: McGill-Queen's Press.

Margutti, Adriana, Cláudia de Pinho, and Karla Oliveira. n.d. "Povos e Comunidades Tradicionais: Os guardiões da natureza sob ataque." Revista Caminhos. Accessed on March 09, 2021. https://www.revistacaminhos.org/meio-ambiente-ovos-e-comunidades-tradicionais-os-guardioes-da-natureza-sob-ataque

Marques, Gilberto. 2007. "Estado e desenvolvimento na Amazônia: a inclusão amazônica na reprodução capitalista brasileira." Ph.D. diss., Universidade Federal Rural do Rio De Janeiro, Instituto e Ciências Humanas e Sociais Curso Pós-Graduação Em Desenvolvimento, Agricultura e Sociedade. https://institucional.ufrrj.br/portalcpda/files/2018/08/2007.tese_.gilberto_de_souza_marques.pdf

Marques, Gilberto. 2012. "Amazônia: Uma moderna colônia energético mineral." *Ciência & Tecnologia* 49: 32–45.

Martinez-Alier, Joan. 2002. *The Environmentalism of the Poor: A Study of Ecological Conflicts and Aaluation*. Cheltenham, UK: Edward Elgar.

Martins, José de Souza. 1984. *A militarização da questão agraria no Brasil [terra e poder]: o problema da terra na crise politica*. Petrópolis, Brazil: Vozes.

Marx, Karl. 1976 [1867]. *Capital: A Critique of Political Economy. Volume I. Book One: The Process of Production of Capital*. Translation by Ben Fowkes. London, UK: Penguin.

May, Peter H., ed. 1999. *Natural Resource Valuation and Policy in Brazil: Methods and Cases*. New York, NY: Columbia University Press.

Mbembe, Achille. 2019. "Necropolitics." In *Foucault in an Age of Terror: Essays on Biopolitics and the Defence of Society*, edited by Stephen Morton and Stephen Bygrave. 152–182. London, UK: Palgrave Macmillan. https://doi.org/10.1057/9780230584334_9

McBrien Justin. 2016. "Accumulating extinction: planetary catastrophism in the necrocene." In *Anthropocene or Capitalocene?: Nature, History, and the Crisis of Capitalism*, edited by Jason W. Moore. 116–137. Oakland, CA: PM Press.

McCarthy, John F. 2010. "Processes of Inclusion and Adverse Incorporation: Oil Palm and Agrarian Change in Sumatra, Indonesia." *The Journal of Peasant Studies* 37(4): 821–850. https://doi.org/10.1080/03066150.2010.512460

McKay, Ben M. 2017. "Agrarian Extractivism in Bolivia." *World Development* 97: 199–211. https://doi.org/10.1016/j.worlddev.2017.04.007

McKay, Ben M. 2020. *The Political Economy of Agrarian Extractivism: Lessons from Bolivia*. Warwickshire, UK: Practical Action Publishing Limited.

McKay, Ben M., A. Alonso-Fradejas, and A. Ezquerro-Cañete, eds. forthcoming 2021. *Agrarian Extractivism in Latin America*. London, UK: Routledge.

McOwan, Gavin. 2009. "Top 10 Beaches in Brazil," *The Guardian (UK Edition)*, April 15, 2009. https://www.theguardian.com/travel/2009/apr/15/beach-brazil-top-10

Medici Emília P., Fernandes-Santos Renata Carolina, Testa-José Caroline, Godinho Antonio Francisco, and Brand Anne-Fleur. 2021. "Lowland tapir exposure to pesticides and metals in the Brazilian Cerrado." *Wildlife Research*. https://doi.org/10.1071/WR19183

Meinig, D. W. 1986. *The Shaping of America: A Geographical Perspective on 500 Years of History, Vol. 1: Atlantic America, 1492–1800*. New Haven, CT: Yale University Press.

Mezzadra, Sandro, and Brett Neilson. 2019. *The Politics of Operations: Excavating Contemporary Capitalism*. Durham, NC: Duke University Press.

Micarelli, Giovanna, and Helen Verran. 2018. "Two Analyses of Marisol de la Cadena's *Earth Beings: Ecologies of Practice Across Andean worlds.*" *Tapuya: Latin American Science, Technology and Society* 1(1): 123–130. https://doi.org/10.1080/25729861.2018.1543042

Milanez Felipe. 2019. "Countering the order of progress: Colonialism, extractivism and re-existence in the Brazilian Amazon." In *Towards a Political Economy of Degrowth*, edited by Ekaterina Chertkovskaya, Alexander Paulsson, and Stefania Barca. 121–136. London, UK: Rowman & Littlefield International.

Mitchell, Timothy. 2011. *Carbon Democracy: Political Power in the Age of Oil*. New York, NY: Verso.

Mitman, Gregg. 2019. "Reflections on the Plantationocene: A Conversation With Donna Haraway and Anna Tsing," *Edge Effects*, June 18, 2019. https://edgeeffects.net/haraway-tsing-plantationocene/

Mooney, Chris. 2016. "This Huge Region of Brazil is Even More Deforested — and Less Protected — than the Amazon," *Washington Post*, April 4, 2016. https://www.washingtonpost.com/news/energy-environment/wp/2016/04/04/the-amazons-tree-loss-is-bad-but-deforestation-in-this-huge-brazilian-region-is-even-worse/

Moore Jason W. 2014. "The end of cheap nature, or, How I learned to stop worrying about 'the' environment and love the crisis of capitalism." In *Structures of the World Political Economy and the Future of Global Conflict and Cooperation*, edited by Christian Suter and Christopher Chase-Dunn. 285–314. Berlin, Germany: LIT.

Moore, Jason W. 2014. "The Capitalocene Part II: Accumulation by Appropriation and the Centrality of Unpaid Work/Energy." *The Journal of Peasant Studies* 45(2): 237–279. https://doi.org/10.1080/03066150.2016.1272587

Moore, Jason W. 2015. *Capitalism in the Web of Life: Ecology and the Accumulation of Capital*. London: Verso.

Moore, Jason W., ed. 2016. *Anthropocene or Capitalocene?: Nature, History, and the Crisis of Capitalism*. Oakland, CA: PM Press.

Moore, Jason W. 2017a. "Metabolic Rift or Metabolic Shift? Dialectics, Nature, and the World-Historical Method." *Theory and Society* 46(4): 285–318. https://doi.org/10.1007/s11186-017-9290-6

Moore. Jason W. 2017b. "World Accumulation and Planetary Life, or, Why Capitalism will Continue Until the 'Last Tree is Cut." *IPPR Progressive Review* 24(3): 175–202. https://doi.org/10.1111/newe.12055

Muradian, Roldan, and Joan Martinez-Alier. 2001. "Trade and the Environment From a "Southern" perspective." *Ecological Economics* 36(2): 281–297. https://doi.org/10.1016/S0921-8009(00)00229-9

Murphy, Michael Warren, and Caitlin Schroering. 2020. "Refiguring the Plantationocene." *Journal of World-Systems Research* 26(2): 400–415. https://doi.org/10.5195/jwsr.2020.983

Navarro Trujillo, Mina Lorena. 2020. "Struggles in Defense of Life Within the Context of Dispossession and Capitalist Violence in Mexico: A Closer Look Through the Lens of the Production of the Common." *Latin American and Caribbean Ethnic Studies*. 1–20. https://doi.org/10.1080/17442222.2020.1854367

Nepstad, Daniel, David McGrath, Ane Alencar, A. C. Barros, Georgia Carvalho, Mario Santilli, and M. del C. Vera Diaz. 2002. "Frontier Governance in Amazonia." *Science* 295(5555): 629–631. https://doi.org/10.1126/science.1067053

Nepstad, Daniel, Stephan Schwartzman, Barbara Bamberger, Marcio Santilli, Duncan Ray, Peter Schlesinger, Paul Lefebvre, et al. 2006. "Inhibition of Amazon Deforestation and Fire by Parks and Indigenous Lands." *Conservation Biology* 20(1): 65–73. https://doi.org/10.1111/j.1523-1739.2006.00351.x

Nichols, Robert. 2020. *Theft Is Property!: Dispossession and Critical Theory*. Durham, NC: Duke University Press.

Nolte, Christoph, Yann le Polain de Waroux, Jacob Munger, Tiago N.P. Reis, and Eric F. Lambin. 2017. "Conditions Influencing the Adoption of Effective Anti-Deforestation Policies in South America's Commodity Frontiers." *Global Environmental Change* 43: 1–14. https://doi.org/10.1016/j.gloenvcha.2017.01.001

Oliveira, Ariovaldo Umbelino. 2010. "A questão de aquisição de terras por estrangeiros no Brasil – um retorno aos dossiês." *Agrária* 12: 3–113. https://doi.org/10.11606/issn.1808-1150.v0i12p3-113

Oliveira, Gustavo, and Susanna Hecht. 2016. "Sacred Groves, Sacrifice Zones and Soy Production: Globalization, Intensification and Neo-Nature in South America." *The Journal of Peasant Studies* 43(2): 251–85. https://doi.org/10.1080/03066150.2016.1146705

Oliveira, Gustavo de L. T., and Mindi Schneider. 2016. "The Politics of Flexing Soybeans: China, Brazil and Global Agroindustrial Restructuring." *The Journal of Peasant Studies* 43(1): 167–194. https://doi.org/10.1080/03066150.2014.993625

Ollinaho, Ossi I. 2016. "Environmental Destruction as (Objectively) Uneventful and (Subjectively) Irrelevant." *Environmental Sociology* 2(1): 53–63. https://doi.org/10.1080/23251042.2015.1114207

Ollinaho, Ossi, and Markus Kröger. 2021. "Agroforestry Transitions: The Good, the Bad and the Ugly." *Journal of Rural Studies* 82, 210–221. https://doi.org/10.1016/j.jrurstud.2021.01.016

Patel, Raj 2009. "Food Sovereignty." *The Journal of Peasant Studies* 36(3), 663–706. https://doi.org/10.1080/03066150903143079

Patel, Raj, and Jason W. Moore. 2017. *A History of the World in Seven Cheap Things: A Guide to Capitalism, Nature, and the Future of the Planet*. Oakland, CA: University of California Press.

Patomäki, Heikki. 2017. *Disintegrative Tendencies in Global Political Economy: Exits and Conflicts* London, UK: Routledge. https://doi.org/10.4324/9781315159799

Pedlowski, Marcos. 2017. "O explosivo desmatamento na Amazônia brasileira e suas múltiplas consequências sociais e ambientais." *Política científica e sociedade blog do Pedlowski*. July 13, 2017. https://blogdopedlowski.com/2017/07/13/o-explosivo-desmatamento-na-amazonia-brasileira-e-suas-multiplas-consequencias-sociais-e-ambientais/

Pedlowski, Marcos. 2021. "Observatório DOS Agrotóxicos: Com mais 67 liberações, governo Bolsonaro lançou 1.100 agrotóxicos no mercado brasileiro." *Política científica e sociedade blog do Pedlowski*. February 27, 2021. https://blogdopedlowski.com/2021/02/27/observatorio-dos-agrotoxicos-com-mais-67-liberacoes-governo-bolsonaro-lancou-1-100-agrotoxicos-no-mercado-brasileiro/

Penfield Amy. 2019. "Extractive pluralities: The intersection of oil wealth and informal gold mining in venezuelan amazonia." In: *Indigenous Life Projects and Extractivism. Approaches to Social Inequality and Difference*, edited by Cecilie Vindal Ødegaard and Juan Javier Rivera Andía. 75–93. London, UK: Palgrave McMillian.

Penido, Ana, and Mariana da Gama Janot. 2021. *"Dois anos depois, 10 teses e 10 mitos sobre as forças armadas e Bolsonaro," Brasil de Fato* (São Paulo). March 9, 2021. https://www.brasildefato.com.br/2021/03/09/artigo-dois-anos-depois-10-teses-e-10-mitos-sobre-as-forcas-armadas-e-bolsonaro

Perlin, John. 2005. *A Forest Journey: The Story of Wood and Civilization*. Woodstock, VT: The Countryman Press.

Petras, James, and Henry Veltmeyer, eds. 2014. *Extractive Imperialism in the Americas: Capitalism's New Frontier*. Leiden, UK: Brill. https://doi.org/10.1163/9789004268869

Pohjanmies, Tähti, Kyle Eyvindson, María Triviño, Jan Bengtsson, and Mikko Mönkkönen. 2021. "Forest Multifunctionality is not Resilient to Intensive Forestry." *European Journal of Forest Research*: 1–13. https://doi.org/10.1007/s10342-020-01348-7

Polanyi, Karl. 2001. *The Great Transformation. The Political and Economic Origins of our Time*. Boston, MA: Beacon Press.

Polo Blanco, Jorge, and Eleder Piñeiro Aguiar. 2019 "Ciencia moderna, planeta torturado Una reflexión crítica sobre el modo eurocéntrico de conocer la naturaleza e intervenir en el medio ambiente." *Izquierdas (Santiago, Chile)* 46: 194–217. http://dx.doi.org/10.4067/S0718-50492019000200194

Porto-Gonçalves, Carlos Walter. 2006. "A Reinvenção dos Territórios: A experiência latino-americana e caribenha" In *Los desafíos de las emancipaciones en un contexto militarizado*. 151–197. Buenos Aires, Argentina: Consejo Latinoamericano de Ciencias Sociales (CLACSO).

Porto-Gonçalves, Carlos Walter, and Pedro Catanzaro da Rocha Leão. 2020. "Terra, violência e conflito na formação territorial brasileira: Tensões territoriais na Ruptura Política (2015–2019)." *Revista da ANPEGE* 16(29): 706–761.

Raftopoulos, Malayna, and Joanna Morley. 2020. "Ecocide in the Amazon: The Contested Politics of Environmental Rights in Brazil." *The International Journal of Human Rights* 24(10): 1616–1641. https://doi.org/10.1080/13642987.2020.1746648

Ranta, Eija M. 2018. *Vivir Bien as an Alternative to Neoliberal Globalization: Can Indigenous Terminologies Decolonize the State?* London, UK: Routledge. https://doi.org/10.4324/9781315180441

Rasmussen, Mattias Borg, and Christian Lund. 2018. "Reconfiguring Frontier Spaces: The Territorialization of Resource Control." *World Development* 101(C): 388–399. https://doi.org/10.1016/j.worlddev.2017.01.018

Rede Cerrado. n.d. "Mato Grosso: The steamroller." Rede Cerrado. Accessed March 24, 2021. https://redecerrado.org.br/historiasdocerrado/en/mato-grosso/

RedGe Peru. 2017. "Territorios de monocultura y existencias múltiples." June 5, 2017. YouTube Video, 10:26. https://youtu.be/LbFylBvzHy8

Reggio, Godfrey. 1982. *Koyaanisqatsi: Life Out of Balance*. United States: Island Alive.

Rekow, Lea. 2019. "Socio-Ecological Implications of Soy in the Brazilian Cerrado." *Challenges in Sustainability* 7(1): 7–29.

Reydon, B., V. Fernandes, and T. Telles. 2015. "Land Tenure in Brazil: The Question of Regulation and Governance." *Land Use Policy* 42: 509–516. https://doi.org/10.1016/j.landusepol.2014.09.007

Rifkin, Mark. 2017. *Beyond Settler Time: Temporal Sovereignty and Indigenous Self-Determination*. Durham, NC: Duke University Press.

Riofrancos, Thea. 2020. *Resource Radicals: From Petro-Nationalism to Post-Extractivism in Ecuador*. Durham, NC: Duke University Press. https://doi.org/10.2307/j.ctv14t48kg

RRI (Rights and Resources Initiative). 2014. "Lots of Words, Little Action: Will the Private Sector Tip the Scales For Community Land Rights?" Media Campaign. May 2, 2014. https://rightsandresources.org/lots-of-words-little-action-will-the-private-sector-tip-the-scales-for-community-land-rights/

Rivera Andía, Juan Javier, and Cecilie Vindal Ødegaard. 2019. "Introduction: Indigenous Peoples, Extractivism, and Turbulences in South America." In *Indigenous Life Projects and Extractivism. Approaches to Social Inequality and Difference*, edited by Cecilie Vindal Ødegaard and Juan Javier Rivera Andía. 1–50. London, UK: Palgrave McMillian. https://doi.org/10.1007/978-3-319-93435-8_1

Rose, Deborah Bird. 2011. *Wild Dog Dreaming: Love and Extinction*. Charlottesville, VA: University of Virginia Press.

Rose, Deborah Bird, Thom van Dooren, and Matthew Chrulew, eds. 2017. *Extinction Studies: Stories of Time, Death, and Generations*. New York, NY: Columbia University Press.

Rosing, Minik, Rebekka Knudsen, Jens Heinrich, and Lars Rasmussen. 2014. *To the Benefit of Greenland. The Committee for Greenlandic Mineral Resources to the Benefit of Society*. Nuussuaq, Greenland: Ilisimatusarfik, University of Greenland.

Rozzi, Ricardo. 2018. "Biocultural homogenization: A wicked problem in the anthropocene." In *From Biocultural Homogenization to Biocultural Conservation*, edited by Ricardo Rizzo, Roy H. May, Jr., F. Stuart Chapin, III, Francisca Massardo, Michael C. Gavin, Irene J. Klaver, Aníbal Pauchard,

Martin A. Nuñez, and Daniel Simberloff, 21–48. New York, NY: Springer International Publishing.

Saes, Beatriz Macchione, and Arpita Bisht. 2020. "Iron Ore Peripheries in the Extractive Boom: A Comparison Between Mining Conflicts in India and Brazil." *The Extractive Industries and Society* 7(4): 1567–1578. https://doi.org/10.1016/j.exis.2020.09.010

Sauer, Sérgio, and Sergio Pereira Leite. 2012. "Agrarian Structure, Foreign Investment in Land, and Land Prices In Brazil." *The Journal of Peasant Studies* 39: 873–98. https://doi.org/10.1080/03066150.2012.686492

Schmink, Marianne, and Charles H. Wood. 1992. *Contested Frontiers in Amazonia*. New York, NY: Columbia University Press.

Scott, Dayna Nadine. 2020. "Extractivism: Socio-legal Approaches to Relations with Lands and Resources." Forthcoming in *Handbook of Law and Society*. https://digitalcommons.osgoode.yorku.ca/scholarly_works/2811

Shapiro, Judith, and John-Andrew McNeish, eds. 2021. *Our Hyper-extractive Age: Expressions of Violence and Resistance*. London, UK: Routledge.

Shattuck, Annie. 2021. "Generic, Growing, Green?: The Changing Political Economy of the Global Pesticide Complex." *The Journal of Peasant Studies* 49(2): 231–253. https://doi.org/10.1080/03066150.2020.1839053

Signatories. 2021. Open Letter to Editors of Jacobin and Monthly Review, *New Politics*. March 2, 2021. https://newpol.org/open-letter-to-editors-of-jacobin-and-monthly-review/

Siikala, Anna-Leena. 1992. *Suomalainen šamanismi: mielikuvien historiaa*. Helsinki, Finland: Suomalaisen kirjallisuuden seura.

Silva-Santisteban, Rocío, ed. 2020. *Indigenous Women & Climate Change*. Lima, Peru: IWGIA.

Singer, Peter. 1995. *Animal Liberation*. New York, NY: Random House.

Smith, Neil. 2003. *American Empire: Roosevelt's Geographer and the Prelude to Globalization*. Berkeley, CA: University of California Press.

Smith, Neil. 2008 [1984]. *Uneven Development: Nature, Capital and the Production of Space*. Athens, GA: The University of Georgia Press.

SOSOrinoco. 2021. "Documental: El Arco Minero ¿Ecocidio o Suicidio?" February 1, 2021. YouTube Video, 19:24. https://youtu.be/YmrtyC95ovw.

Soterroni, Aline C., Fernando M. Ramos, Aline Mosnier, Joseph Fargione, Pedro R. Andrade, Leandro Baumgarten, Johannes Pirker, et al. 2019. "Expanding the Soy Moratorium to Brazil's Cerrado." *Science Advances* 5(7): eaav7336. https://doi.org/10.1126/sciadv.aav7336

Souza Jessé. 2019. *A elite do atraso: da escravidão a Bolsonaro*. Estação, Brasil: Estação, Brasil.

Soyer, Gabriel, and Ricardo Barbosa, Jr. 2020. "O extrativismo agrário do Governo Bolsonaro a partir das relações Estado-Sociedade." *Revista da ANPEGE* 16(29): 516–548. https://doi.org/10.5418/ra2020.v16i29.12553

Spera, Stephanie A., Gillian L. Galford, Michael T. Coe, Marcia N. Macedo, and John F. Mustard. 2016. "Land-Use Change Affects Water Recycling in Brazil's Last Agricultural Frontier." *Global Change Biology* 22(10): 3405–3413. https://doi.org/10.1111/gcb.13298

Stensrud Astrid B. 2019. "Water as resource and being: Water extractivism and life projects in Peru." In *Indigenous Life Projects and Extractivism. Approaches to Social Inequality and Difference*, edited by Cecilie Vindal Ødegaard and Juan Javier Rivera Andía. 143–164. London, UK: Palgrave McMillian.

Stop Ecocide. n.d. "FAQs – Ecocide and the Law." https://www.stopecocide.earth/

Svampa, Maristella. 2019. *Neo-Extractivism in Latin America: Socio-Environmental Conflicts, the Territorial Turn, and New Political Narratives*. Cambridge, UK: Cambridge University Press.

Talve, Ilmar. 1990. *Suomen kansankulttuuri*. Helsinki, Finland: Suomalaisen kirjallisuuden seura.

Tarlau, Rebecca. 2019. *Occupying Schools, Occupying Land: How the Landless Workers Movement Transformed Brazilian Education*. New York, NY: Oxford University Press. https://doi.org/10.1093/oso/9780190870324.001.0001

Taylor, Marcus. 2015. *The Political Ecology of Climate Change Adaptation: Livelihoods, Agrarian Change and the Conflicts of Development*. London, UK: Routledge.

Thompson, Edward Palmer. 1963. *The Making of the English Working Class*. New York, NY: Random House Books.

Thompson, Edward Palmer. 1971. "The Moral Economy of the English Crowd in the Eighteenth Century." *Past and Present* 50(1): 76–136. https://doi.org/10.1093/past/50.1.76

Thomson, Ashley. 2020. "Biodiversity and the Amazon Rainforest." Greenpeace. May 22, 2020. https://www.greenpeace.org/usa/biodiversity-and-the-amazon-rainforest/

Toivanen, Tero. 2018. "Pohjoinen polku kapitalismin ympäristöhistoriaan: Tervakapitalismi, yhteisvauraus ja sosioekologinen mullistus 1800-luvun Kainuussa." Ph.D. diss., University of Helsinki. https://helda.helsinki.fi/handle/10138/253843

Toivanen, Tero, and Markus Kröger. 2019. "The Role of Debt, Death and Dispossession in World-Ecological Transformations: Swidden Commons and Tar Capitalism in Nineteenth-Century Finland." *The Journal of Peasant Studies* 46(7), 1368–1388. https://doi.org/10.1080/03066150.2018.1503173

Tollefson, Jeff. 2020. "Why Deforestation and Extinctions Make Pandemics More Likely," *Nature News*, August 7, 2020. https://www.nature.com/articles/d41586-020-02341-1

Trouillaud, Pascale. 2020. "To 11 Million Brazilians, the Earth is flat," *The Jakarta Post*, February 28, 2020. https://www.thejakartapost.com/life/2020/02/28/to-11-million-brazilians-the-earth-is-flat.html

Truscello, Michael. 2020. *Infrastructural Brutalism. Art and the Necropolitics of Infrastructure*. Cambridge, MA: MIT Press. https://doi.org/10.7551/mitpress/10905.001.0001

Tsing, Anna Lowenhaupt. 2015. *The Mushroom at the End of the World: On the Possibility of life in Capitalist Ruins*. Princeton, NJ: Princeton University Press.

Tsing, Anna. 2018. "On Nonscalability: The Living World Is Not Amenable to Precision-Nested Scales." *Common Knowledge* 18(3):143–162. https://doi.org/10.1215/0961754X-1630424

Turner, Frederick Jackson. 1893. "The Significance of the Frontier in American History." *The Proceedings of the American Historical Association for 1893*, 199–222. Reprinted in 2010 in *The Frontier in American History*. Mineola, NY: Dover Publications.

Turner, Terence. 2008. "Marxian Value Theory: An Anthropological Perspective." *Anthropological Theory* 8(1), 43–56. https://doi.org/10.1177/1463499607087494

Ulloa, Astrid. 2020. "The Rights of the Wayúu People and Water in the Context of Mining in La Guajira, Colombia: Demands of Relational Water Justice." *Human Geography* 13(1): 6–15. https://doi.org/10.1177/1942778620910894.

UOL Notícias. 2010. "Leia a íntegra do discurso do presidente Lula no lançamento do PAC 2." Do UOL Notícias. March 29, 2010. http://noticias.uol.com.br/especiais/pac/ultnot/2010/03/29/leia-a-integra-do-discurso-do-presidente-lula-no-lancamento-do-pac-2.jhtm

van Apeldoorn, Bastiaan, Naná de Graaff, and Henk Overbeek 2012. "The Rebound of the Capitalist State: The Rearticulation of the State-Capital Nexus in the Global Crisis." *Globalizations* 9(4): 467–470. https://doi.org/10.1080/14747731.2012.699960

Vanzolini, Marina, and Pedro Cesarino. 2014. *Perspectivism*. Oxford Bibliographies Online in Anthropology. DOI:10.1093/obo/9780199766567-0083

Veltmeyer, Henry, and James Petras. 2014. *The New Extractivism: A Post-Neoliberal Development Model or Imperialism of the Twenty-First Century?* London, UK: Zed Books.

Viveiros de Castro, Eduardo. 2004. "Perspectival Anthropology and the Method of Controlled Equivocation." *Tipití: Journal of the Society for the Anthropology of Lowland South America* 2(1): 3–22. https://digitalcommons.trinity.edu/tipiti/vol2/iss1/1

Viveiros de Castro, Eduardo. 2012. *Cosmological Perspectivism in Amazonia and Elsewhere*. London, UK: HAU Books.

Walker, Richard A. 2001. "California's golden road to riches: natural resources and regional capitalism, 1848–1940." *Annals of the Association of American Geographers* 91(1): 167–199. https://doi.org/10.1111/0004-5608.00238

Walker, Robert, John Browder, Eugenio Arima, Cynthia Simmons, Ritaumaria Pereira, Marcellus Caldas, Ricardo Shirota, and Sergio de Zene. 2009. "Ranching and the New Global Range: Amazônia in the 21st Century." *Geoforum* 40(5): 732–745. https://doi.org/10.1016/j.geoforum.2008.10.009

Walker, Richard, and Jason W. Moore. 2019. "Value, nature, and the vortex of accumulation." In *Urban Political Ecology in the Anthropo-Obscene: Interruptions and Possibilities*, edited by Henrik Ernstson and Erik Swyngedouw. 48–68. London, UK: Routledge. https://doi.org/10.4324/9781315210537-3

Wallerstein, Immanuel. 2011. "Structural Crisis in the World-System: Where Do We Go from Here?" *Monthly Review* 62(10). https://doi.org/10.14452/MR-062-10-2011-03_2

Wallerstein, Immanuel, Randall Collins, Michael Mann, Georgi Derluguian, and Craig Calhoun, eds. 2013. *Does Capitalism Have a Future?* New York, NY: Oxford University Press.

Wallerstein, Immanuel. 2013. "Structural Crisis or Why Capitalists May No Longer Find Capitalism Rewarding." In *Does Capitalism Have a Future?*, edited by Immanuel Wallerstein, Randall Collins, Michael Mann, Georgi Derluguian, and Craig Calhoun. 9–36. New York, NY: Oxford University Press.

Wanderley, Luiz Jardim, Ricardo Junior de Assis Fernandes Gonçalves, and Bruno Milanez. 2020. "O interesse é no minério: o neoextrativismo ultraliberal marginal e a ameaça de expansão da fronteira mineral pelo governo Bolsonaro." *Revista da ANPEGE* 16(29): 555–559. https://doi.org/10.5418/ra2020.v16i29.12457.

Watts, Jonathan. 2017. "Brazil Abolishes Huge Amazon Reserve in "Biggest Attack" in 50 Years," *The Guardian*, August 24, 2017. https://www.theguardian.com/environment/2017/aug/24/brazil-abolishes-huge-amazon-reserve-in-biggest-attack-in-50-years

Weis, Anthony John. 2013. *The Ecological Hoofprint: The Global Burden of Industrial Livestock*. London, UK: Zed Books.

Weisman Alan. 2007 *The World Without Us*. New York, NY: St. Martin's Thomas Dunne Books.

Weissheimer, Marco. 2016. "Água, ar e leite materno contaminado: pesquisa no MT expõe impacto dos agrotóxicos," *Sul21*. February 9, 2016. https://www.sul21.com.br/areazero/2016/02/agua-ar-e-leite-materno-contaminado-pesquisa-no-mt-expoe-impacto-dos-agrotoxicos/

White, Ben, Saturnino M. Borras, Jr., Ruth Hall, Ian Scoones, and Wendy Wolford. 2012 "The New Enclosures: Critical Perspectives on Corporate Land Deals." *The Journal of Peasant Studies* 39(3–4), 619–647. https://doi.org/10.1080/03066150.2012.691879

Willow, Anna J. 2019. *Understanding ExtrACTIVISM: Culture and Power in Natural Resource Disputes*. New York, NY: Routledge.

Winders Bill, and Elizabeth Ransom. 2019. *Global Meat: Social and Environmental Consequences of the Expanding Meat Industry*. Cambridge, MA: The MIT Press. https://doi.org/10.7551/mitpress/11868.001.0001

Wolford. Wendy. 2021 "The Plantationocene: A Lusotropical Contribution to the Theory." *Annals of the American Association of Geographers*. https://doi.org/10.1080/24694452.2020.1850231

Wolford, Wendy. 2010. *This Land is Ours Now: Social Mobilization and the Meanings of Land in Brazil*. Durham, NC: Duke University Press.

Woodley, Daniel. 2015. *Globalization and Capitalist Geopolitics: Sovereignty and State Power in a Multipolar World*. New York, NY: Routledge.

World Health Organization (WHO). 2016. IARC Monograph on Glyphosate. March 1, 2016 Retrieved March 08, 2021, from https://www.iarc.who.int/featured-news/media-centre-iarc-news-glyphosate/

Wright, Erik Olin. 2005. "Foundations of a neo-Marxist class analysis." In *Approaches to Class Analysis*, edited by Erik Olin Wright. 4–30. Cambridge, UK: Cambridge University Press.

WWF (World Wildlife Fund). 2020. *Living Planet Report 2020 - Bending the Curve of Biodiversity Loss*, edited by Rosamunde E.A. Almond, Monique Grooten, and Tanya Petersen. Gland, Switzerland: WWF. https://livingplanet.panda.org/en-us/

Ye, Jingzhong, Jan Douwe van der Ploeg, Sergio Schneider, and Teodor Shanin. 2020. "The Incursions of Extractivism: Moving From Dispersed Places to Global Capitalism." *The Journal of Peasant Studies* 47(1), 155–183. https://doi.org/10.1080/03066150.2018.1559834

Young, Carlos Eduardo Frickmann. 2017. "Por um punhado de cobres: mineração e retrocesso na Amazônia." Qualidade da Democracia. August 28, 2017. https://qualidadedademocracia.com.br/por-um-punhado-de-cobres-minera%C3%A7%C3%A3o-e-retrocesso-na-amaz%C3%B4nia-2288f03b4f19

Zabyelina, Yulija, and Dan van Uhm. 2020. "The new Eldorado: organized crime, informal mining, and the global scarcity of metals and minerals." In *Illegal Mining: Organized Crime, Corruption, and Ecocide in a Resource-Scarce World*, edited by Yulija Zabyelina and Dan van Uhm. London, UK: Palgrave Macmillan. https://doi.org/10.1007/978-3-030-46327-4

Zenni, Rafael Dudeque, Rafaela Guimarães, and Rosana Tidon. 2019. "Biotic Homogenization of the South American Cerrado." In *From Biocultural Homogenization to Biocultural Conservation. Ecology and Ethics, Vol 3*, edited by Ricardo Rozzi, Roy H. May, Jr., F. Stuart Chapin, III, Francisca Massardo, Michael C. Gavin, Irene J. Klaver, Aníbal Pauchard, Martin A. Nuñez, and Daniel Simberloff. 265–274. Cham, Switzerland: Springer. https://doi.org/10.1007/978-3-319-99513-7_16

Zhouri, Andréa. 2010. "'Adverse Forces' in the Brazilian Amazon: Developmentalism Versus Environmentalism and Indigenous Rights." *The Journal of Environment & Development* 19(3): 252–273. https://doi.org/10.1177/1070496510378097.

# Index

For Product Safety Concerns and Information please contact our EU
representative GPSR@taylorandfrancis.com
Taylor & Francis Verlag GmbH, Kaufingerstraße 24, 80331 München, Germany

www.ingramcontent.com/pod-product-compliance
Ingram Content Group UK Ltd.
Pitfield, Milton Keynes, MK11 3LW, UK
UKHW022344190926
475702UK00015B/2094
* 9 7 8 0 3 6 7 6 1 0 3 3 3 *